GREEK FOLK RELIGION

DEMETER, TRIPTOLEMOS, AND KORE

GREEK FOLK RELIGION

MARTIN P. NILSSON

WITH A FOREWORD BY ARTHUR DARBY NOCK

UNIVERSITY OF PENNSYLVANIA PRESS

PHILADELPHIA

Copyright 1940 by Columbia University Press

Printed in the United States of America

Foreword Copyright © 1961 by Arthur Darby Nock

This volume was first published under the title GREEK POPULAR RELIGION by the Columbia University Press, New York, in 1940.

Fifth paperback printing, 1987

ISBN: 0–8122–1034–4

FOREWORD

This book contains lectures which were delivered in 1939–40 at many points in the United States, that on the Religion of Eleusis being under the auspices of the Norton Lectureship of the Archaeological Institute of America and the rest being under those of the American Council of Learned Societies. Appearing in 1940 (under the title *Greek Popular Religion*), it at once took its place as something unique in the extensive literature relating to ancient religion. It has been translated into French and modern Greek, and after twenty years it retains all its freshness.

A Swedish proverb speaks of placing the church in the middle of the village, and that is precisely what Nilsson has here done. Homer and Hesiod formed the basis of the traditional education of the Greeks in general, and the great gods and goddesses as they appear in art show at all times the formative influence of the epic tradition. Nevertheless, the hard core of Greek religion is to be found in its observances: these took their shape among men whose focus was first the hearth and then the city-state, men moreover whose life and livelihood were tied to crops and herds and the annual cycle of nature. Urbanization brought changes, but we must not make too much of them, for in Greece proper there never was a cosmopolitan city like Alexandria and even the Athenians did not wholly lose touch with the good brown earth.

Furthermore, the adventures of ideas which mark the second half of the fifth century B.C. and which so profoundly

affected later European thinking should not lead us to think
of the Greeks in general as being or becoming in any very
large measure like men of the Enlightenment. After all, in
413 a lunar eclipse caused the majority of the Athenians
serving before Syracuse to urge Nicias and his fellow generals
to delay a departure in which lay their only hope. It is therefore most important to be reminded of the immense part
which oracles and methods of divination played in Greek life.
These things counted for so much. So did various forms of
fear and superstition; as a rule they were not obsessive, but
they were present and could make themselves felt. You cannot understand the Greek achievement in poetry and philosophy if you ignore its background in religion at a popular level.

Nilsson has no equal today, and has, I think, never had an
equal in his capacity to understand and interpret this background. He combines a complete mastery of the ancient
evidence, literary and monumental alike, a thorough familiarity
with the landscape and the seasons of Greece, and a natural
feeling for folkways. This last he has in his blood and,
extensive as is his reading in anthropology, he owes much
more to the generations of ancestors who farmed at Bal-
lingslöv in Southern Sweden.[1] It is no effort for him to recap-
ture Hesiod's world. Let me quote in translation what he has
recently written in answer to friendly criticism of his monumental *Geschichte der griechischen Religion*: 'I have been
criticized for being one-sided. I come from an old line of
peasants who occupied the same farm for two hundred years.
I still know something of how the people thought seventy
years ago, before the full impact of the great transformation.
I know something of the sanctity of bread. When I set about
writing a history of Greek religion, I wanted to find out
what it was in which the peasant on the farm, the shepherd

[1] For a vivid illustration cf. p. 71 below.

on the mountains, and the town-dweller believed. I thought then and I still think today that this too has its place in a history of Greek religion and Greek belief.'

It is such wisdom and understanding which this reprint brings to a wider public.

Arthur Darby Nock

Eliot House, Cambridge, Mass.

ACKNOWLEDGMENTS

ACKNOWLEDGMENT IS HEREBY MADE TO: ALINARI, Kaufmann, and the British Museum for the use of photographs; A. & C. Black, Ltd., for the figure from Dugas, *Greek Pottery*; F. Bruckmann, A.-G., for the figures from Brunn and Bruckmann, *Denkmäler griechischer und römischer Sculptur*, from Furtwängler and Reichhold, *Griechische Vasenmalerei*, and from the *Festschrift für James Loeb zum sechzigsten Geburtstag gewidmet*; Cambridge University Press for the figures from Cook, *Zeus*, and from Harrison, *Prolegomena to the Study of Greek Religion*; Gryphius-Verlag for the figure from Watzinger, *Griechische Vasen in Tübingen*; Libreria dello Stato for the figure from Rizzio, *Monumenti della pittura antica scoperti in Italia*; The Macmillan Company for the figures from Cook, *Zeus*, and from Dugas, *Greek Pottery*; Oxford University Press for the figures from Farnell, *The Cults of the Greek States*, and from Tod and Wace, *A Catalogue of the Sparta Museum*; Vereinigung wissenschaftlicher Verleger for the figure from Bieber, *Die Denkmäler zum Theaterwesen im Altertum*; Verlag der Königlichen Akademie der Wissenschaften for the figure from Hiller von Gaertringen and Lattermann, *Arkadische Forschungen*; B. G. Teubner for the figure from Roscher, *Ausführliches Lexikon der griechischen und römischen Mythologie*; and the editors and directors of the *Annual of the British School at Athens*,

Ephemeris archaiologike, Illustrated London News, Jahres-hefte des Österreichischen archäologischen Institutes in Wien, and *Mitteilungen des Deutschen archäologischen Instituts* for the use of other figures reproduced in this volume.

CONTENTS

FOREWORD, BY ARTHUR DARBY NOCK   vii

THE COUNTRYSIDE   3

Lines of research in the study of Greek religion; importance of popular religion; agriculture and stockbreeding the foundations of Greek life in early times; Zeus, the weather god; weather magic; human sacrifices to Zeus Lykaios and to Zeus Laphystios; prayers for rain; stone heaps and their god, Hermes; stone heaps as tombs—Hermes Psychopompos; the herms; pastoral gods—Pan; the rivers and their gods—represented in the form of a bull or a horse; Poseidon, the god of water and earthquakes; centaurs; seilenoi and satyrs; nymphs; Artemis, the foremost of the nymphs; the Nereids in modern Greek belief; the sacral landscape; the heroes; sometimes the heroes appear as ghosts; cult of the heroes bound to their tombs and relics; transference of the relics; heroes helpful in everything, but especially in war; similarity of hero cult to the cult of the saints; the great gods less prominent in the rustic cults; the great gods disappeared, while rustic beliefs survived

RURAL CUSTOMS AND FESTIVALS   22

Greece originally, and still in part, a country of peasants, who cling to old customs; Greek mode of living; significance of agriculture in the festivals; a natural calendar; Demeter, the Corn Mother, and her festivals; festival of autumn sowing—the Thesmophoria; festivals of harvest—the Thalysia and the Kalamaia; the preharvest festival—the Thargelia—and the pharmakos; first fruits and their significance; the bucoliasts; the panspermia and the kernos; cultivation of the olive; the gardening festival—the Haloa; the flower festival—the Anthesteria —the blessing of the new wine, and the Athenian All Souls' Day; vintage festivals; Dionysus and the wine; the phallus; the May bough—the eiresione; the boys carry swallows; other forms of the May branch—the thyrsus and the crown; tenacity of rural customs

THE RELIGION OF ELEUSIS 42

Eleusinian religion, the highest form of Greek popular religion; scanty knowledge of the mystery rites; unreliability of the accounts by Christian authors; modern interpretations referring to sexual symbols; our knowledge of the deities and of the myths; Mycenaean origin of the Eleusinian cult; two triads—Demeter, Kore, and Triptolemos and "the God" (Plouton), "the Goddess" (Persephone), and Eubouleus; representations in art; *Homeric Hymn to Demeter*; legend of Eubouleus and the sacrifice of the pig; aetiological character of the *Homeric Hymn* referring to the preliminary rites; rape of Kore refers to storing of corn in subterranean silos at time of threshing; Plouton, the god of wealth (the store of corn); fetching of corn at autumn sowing is the ascent of Kore; Plouton as god of the underworld—burial jars; Greek Corn Maiden and pre-Greek queen of the underworld; second ascent of Kore in the sprouting of the new crop; reuniting of Mother and Maid in the autumn sowing is kernel of the mysteries; the ear of corn; Triptolemos, the hero of agriculture and of civilized life; the Eleusinian ideas of peace and piety; happiness in the underworld a repetition of the mystery celebration; sprouting of the new crop a symbol of the eternity of life in successive generations; monuments showing that individual edification came to the fore in the fourth century B.C.; accretion of Dionysiac elements

THE HOUSE AND THE FAMILY 65

Fear of the wilderness; the Greek house (megaron) and its courtyard; Zeus Herkeios, Zeus Kataibates, and Zeus Ktesios; the Dioscuri in the house cult; Zeus Meilichios and Zeus Soter; Zeus, "the father" (pater familias), the protector of the house; the snake guardian of the house; the hearth and its sanctity; rites at the hearth; sanctity of the meal; animal sacrifice; Hestia; the public hearth; intermingling of sacred and profane in daily life; hearth sacred in itself; Zeus, as the protector of suppliants and foreigners, upholds the unwritten laws; averters of evil and witchcraft—Heracles, Apollo Agyieus, Hecate; social aspect of ancient Greek religion; no professional priests; cults the property of certain families; democratization of the family cult

THE CITIES; THE PANEGYREIS 84

Urbanization of Greek life—industry and commerce; the rule of the tyrants; Athenian state religion; religion secularized and the great gods elevated; the handicrafts; the potters' gods; Athena and her decreasing popularity among the common people; Hephaistos; man's need for gods near to him; importation of foreign gods; Hecate, the goddess of witchcraft; specters; the Great Mother, Ammon, the Cabiri, Bendis, Kotyto, and Sabazios; the rise of the cult of Asclepius; the

trials for atheism; the turning away from ancestral gods; popularity
of mystic and orgiastic cults; religion of the women; cult of Adonis;
the panegyreis; the great games, the amphictyonies, and the truces;
the fairs; modern Greek panegyreis; the importance of the panegyreis
for the social and "international" life of the ancient Greeks

LEGALISM AND SUPERSTITION; HELL   102

Religious movements of the early age; mystic and ecstatic forms of religion; union with the god Dionysus; legalism the striving to fulfill the
divine commandments; miracle men; Hesiod's rules for the religious
life and the conduct of man; the Pythagorean maxims; *The Days;*
regulation of the calendar; legalism accepted by Delphi in cult only;
the Seven Sages and Apolline piety; justice, the equalization of rights;
hybris and nemesis; baskania; the gods in the abstract; superstition
and the significance of the word deisidaimonia; Theophrastus' characterization of the deisidaimon; Hecate, the goddess of witchcraft;
Hippocrates' tract on the holy disease; ghost stories; Plato on sorcery;
imprecatory tablets of the fourth century B.C.; general conception of the
nether world; punishment in the underworld, starting from the Orphic
idea that he who has not been purified will "lie in the mud"; demand
for moral purity added; mythological and other sinners; idea of
punishment in the other life promoted by idea of retributive justice;
hell in Aristophanes; spread of the fear of punishment in the other life

SEERS AND ORACLES   121

The religious situation in the fifth and fourth centuries B.C.; belief
shaken but not abandoned; religious hysteria and the trials for
atheism; Greek religion bound up with political life; advice of oracles
sought by the state and by individuals; art of foretelling the future a
part of Greek religion; questions concerning daily life put to the
oracles; role of the seers in war; popularity of the seers; the oracle
mongers and their influence on public opinion; collections of oracles;
political importance of the oracles; *Sibylline Books*; Thucydides'
account of oracles; role of the oracles in the preparation of the expedition to Sicily; oracles in Aristophanes; some seers were influential
politicians; seers the defenders of the old religion; Diopeithes, the
instigator of the trials for atheism; clash between seers' interpretation
of phenomena and that of the natural philosophers; the Sophists confused with the natural philosophers in popular opinion; clash between
belief and disbelief took place not in theoretical discussion but in
practical life

ILLUSTRATIONS   143

INDEX   159

ILLUSTRATIONS

1. DEMETER, TRIPTOLEMOS, AND KORE   *Frontispiece*
   Votive relief. National Museum, Athens (Photograph by Alinari)

2. ARCADIAN HERM   143
   From K. Rhomaios, "Arkadikoi Hermai," *Ephemeris archaiologike,*
   1911

3. HERMES PSYCHOPOMPOS   143
   Lekythos. Jena. From A. Furtwängler and K. Reichhold, *Griechische Vasenmalerei* (Munich, 1900-1932)

4. HERM OFFERING   143
   Red-figured vase. From C. Watzinger, *Griechische Vasen in
   Tübingen* (Reutlingen, 1924)

5. GOAT DAEMONS   144
   Bronze statuette. From F. Hiller von Gaertringen and H. Lattermann, *Arkadische Forschungen* (Berlin, 1911)

6. RIVER GOD   144
   Red-figured vase. Louvre, Paris. From J. E. Harrison, *Prolegomena
   to the Study of Greek Religion,* 3d ed. (Cambridge, 1922)

7. VOTIVE MASKS   144
   Terracotta masks from the shrine of Artemis Orthia. From the
   Illustrated London News, Oct. 17, 1936

8. PAN AND NYMPHS   145
   Votive relief. National Museum, Athens (Photograph by Alinari)

9. LANDSCAPE WITH SHRINES   145
   Fresco. House of Livia, Rome. From G. E. Rizzio, *Monumenti della
   pittura antica scoperti in Italia* (Rome, 1936-38)

10. HERO IN A SHRINE   145
Votive relief. National Museum, Athens (Photograph by Alinari)

11. KERNOS   146
British Museum, London. From "Notes from the Cyclades," *Annual of the British School at Athens,* III (1896-97)

12. SWINGING FESTIVAL   146
Red-figured skyphos. State Museum, Berlin. From A. Furtwängler and K. Reichhold, *Griechische Vasenmalerei* (Munich, 1900-1932)

13. DIONYSUS IN A SHIP   147
Black-figured vase. Bologna. From M. Bieber, *Die Denkmäler zum Theaterwesen im Altertum* (Berlin, 1920)

14. WINE OFFERING TO DIONYSUS   147
Red-figured stamnos. National Museum, Naples. From A. Furtwängler and K. Reichhold, *Griechische Vasenmalerei* (Munich, 1900-1932)

15. INITIATION RITES   148
Marble vase. National Museum, Rome. From L. R. Farnell, *The Cults of the Greek States* (Oxford, 1896-1909)

16. GODS OF ELEUSIS   148
Votive relief. National Museum, Athens. From *Ephemeris archaiologike,* 1886

17. ANODOS OF PHEREPHATTA   149
Red-figured krater. Albertinum Museum, Dresden. From J. E. Harrison, *Prolegomena to the Study of Greek Religion,* 3d ed. (Cambridge, 1922)

18. ANODOS OF KORE   149
Black-figured lekythos. Bibliothèque Nationale, Paris. J. E. Harrison *Prolegomena to the Study of Greek Religion,* 3d ed. (Cambridge, 1922)

19. BEARDED TRIPTOLEMOS   150
Black-figured amphora. From A. B. Cook, *Zeus* (Cambridge, 1914-25)

20. CORN IN A SHRINE   150
Red-figured vase. Hermitage, Leningrad. From P. Wolters, "Die goldenen Ähren," *Festschrift für James Loeb zum sechzigsten Geburtstag gewidmet* (Munich, 1930)

21. REUNION OF DEMETER AND KORE   150
Pinax of Ninnion. Ethnikon Museum, Athens. From L. R. Farnell, *The Cults of the Greek States* (Oxford, 1896-1909)

22. DEPARTURE OF TRIPTOLEMOS   151
Red-figured skyphos by Hieron. British Museum, London. From A. Furtwängler and K. Reichhold, *Griechische Vasenmalerei* (Munich, 1900-1932)

23. TRIPTOLEMOS WITH A PLOW   151
Red-figured skyphos. From J. E. Harrison, *Prolegomena to the Study of Greek Religion*, 3d ed. (Cambridge, 1922)

24. THE CHILD PLOUTON   152
Hydria. Museum, Istanbul. From J. E. Harrison, *Prolegomena to the Study of Greek Religion*, 3d ed. (Cambridge, 1922)

25. PLOUTON AND PERSEPHONE (PHERE-
PHATTA)   152
Red-figured kylix. British Museum, London. From L. R. Farnell, *The Cults of the Greek States* (Oxford, 1896-1909)

26. ZEUS KTESIOS   153
Votive relief. From *Mitteilungen des Kaiserlich deutschen archäologischen Instituts, athenische Abteilung*, Vol. XXXIII (1908)

27. ZEUS MEILICHIOS   153
Votive relief from the Peiraeus. Berlin Museum. From J. E. Harrison, *Prolegomena to the Study of Greek Religion*, 3d ed. (Cambridge, 1922)

28. ZEUS MEILICHIOS   153
Votive relief from the Peiraeus. Berlin Museum. From A. B. Cook, *Zeus* (Cambridge, 1914-25)

29. DIOSCURI   154
Coin from Sparta. From W. H. Roscher, *Ausführliches Lexikon der griechischen und römischen Mythologie* (Leipzig, 1884-1937)

30. APOLLO AGYIEUS   154
Coin. From L. R. Farnell, *The Cults of the Greek States* (Oxford, 1896-1909)

31. DIOSCURI   154
Relief from Sparta. Museum, Sparta. From M. N. Tod and A. J. B. Wace, *A Catalogue of the Sparta Museum* (Oxford, 1906)

32. DIOSCURI COMING TO A MEAL   154
Votive relief. Louvre, Paris (Photograph by Alinari)

33. TRIPLE HECATE   154
Collection of Graf Lamberg. From *Jahreshefte des Osterreichischen archäologischen Institutes in Wien,* Vol. XIII (1910)

34. ATHENA ERGANE   155
Red-figured vase. Caputi Collection, Ruvo. From C. Dugas, *Greek Pottery* (London, 1926)

35. CYBELE, THE GREAT MOTHER   155
Black-figured pelike. British Museum, London (Photograph by the British Museum)

36. BENDIS   155
Votive relief. British Museum, London (Photograph by the British Museum)

37. OFFERING TO ASCLEPIUS   156
Votive relief. Glyptothek, Munich (Photograph by Kaufmann)

38. ASCLEPIUS OF MELOS   156
Marble head. British Museum, London. From H. von Brunn and F. Bruckmann, *Denkmäler griechischer und römischer Sculptur,* 1st Series (Munich, 1888-1900)

39. GARDENS OF ADONIS   156
Red-figured aryballos. Karlsruhe. From A. Furtwängler and K. Reichhold, *Griechische Vasenmalerei* (Munich, 1900-1932)

GREEK FOLK RELIGION

THE COUNTRYSIDE

GREEK RELIGION IN ITS VARIOUS ASPECTS HAS BEEN the subject of numerous investigations. Modern research has progressed along two lines especially, the search for primitive survivals and the study of the literary expressions of religion. The first is attributable to the rise of the science of anthropology since the seventies of the last century. In this science the study of Greek religion, viewed as a direct development from a primitive nature religion, has always taken a prominent place. I need only mention the names of Andrew Lang, Sir James Frazer, and Jane Harrison. While it is true that there were very many relics of primitive religion in Greek religion, it must be remembered that Greece was a highly civilized country and that even its most backward inhabitants were subject to the influence of its culture. It is misleading, therefore, to represent Greek religion as essentially primitive. The primitive elements were modified and overlaid by higher elements through the development of Greek culture. They were survivals and must be treated as such.

The second line of research has been pursued by philologists, who, quite naturally from their point of view, found the highest and most valuable expression of Greek religious thought in the works of the great writers and philosophers. I may recall the names of such men as Lewis Campbell, James Adam, and Wilamowitz-Moellendorff. The philologists neglect or impatiently brush aside the popular aspects of Greek religion as less valuable and less well known. It is true that the religion of the masses was on a lower level than the religious ideas of eminent literary men, but it is also true that those ideas made hardly any impression on the development of Greek religion. The writers were not prophets, and the philosophers were seekers of wisdom, not of religious truth. The fate of religion is determined by the masses. The masses are, indeed, susceptible to high religious ideas if they are carried away by a religious genius, but only one such genius arose in Greece, Plato. Even he wished to be regarded as a philosopher rather than as a prophet, and he was accepted as such by his contemporaries. The religious importance of his thought did not come to the fore until half a millennium after his death, although since that time all religions have been subject to his influence.

I should perhaps mention a third kind of inquiry which has been taken up by scholars in recent years, especially in Germany. Their endeavors cannot properly be called research, however, for they have been directed to the systematizing of the religious ideas of the Greeks and the creation of a kind of theology, or, as the authors themselves express it, to revealing the intrinsic and lasting values of Greek religion. To this class belong, among others, W. F. Otto and E. Peterich. The great risk they run is that of imputing to the Greeks a systematization such as is found in religions which have laid down their creeds in books. The Greeks had religious ideas, of course, but they never made them into a system. What the Greeks called theology was either metaphysics, or the doctrine of the persons and works of the various gods.[1]

It is of the greatest importance to attain a well-founded knowledge of Greek popular religion, for the fate of Greek religion as a whole depended on it. It is incorrect to say that we have not the means to acquire such knowledge, for the

---

[1] Θεολογία is πρώτη φιλοσοφία, Aristotle, *Metaphysica*, X, p. 1064a, ll. 33 ff. The persons and the works of the gods are described by Cornutus in a book entitled Ἐπιδρομὴ τῶν κατὰ τὴν ἑλληνικὴν θεολογίαν παραδεδομένων.

means are at hand: first, in our information about the cults in which the piety of believers expressed itself; second, in hints by the writers of the classical period; and third, in archaeological discoveries. As I have stated, we ought not to mistake the popular religion for the primitive elements, which persisted in great measure but were subject to and influenced by the development of Greek civilization and political life.

In beginning my exposition of Greek popular religion I want to draw attention to a point of primary importance. In the latter part of the archaic age and in the classical age the leading cities of Greece were more and more industrialized and commercialized. Greek civilization was urban. Many parts of Greece, however, remained in a backward state, and while they are of no importance in the history of civilization and political life, they are important in the history of religion. For they still preserved the mode of life which had been common in earlier times, when the inhabitants of Greece were peasants, compelled to subsist on the products of their own country—the crops, the fruits, the flocks, and the herds.

In trying to understand Greek popular religion we must start from the agricultural and pastoral life of the countryside, which was neither very advanced nor very primitive culturally. The Greek peasant usually lived in a large village. Many ancient cities with names familiar in history were but villages similar to those found in Greece today. Let us imagine a Greek peasant. He rose early, as simple people always do, before dawn. In the dusk of the morning he looked for the stars which were beginning to wane above the eastern horizon, where the growing light announced the rising of the sun. The stars were for him only indications of the time of the year, not objects of worship. He greeted the rising sun with a kiss of the hand, as he greeted the first swallow or the first kite, but he did not pay it any reverence. He needed rain, and sometimes cool weather, more than he needed the sun. He looked at the highest mountaintop in the neighborhood. Maybe it wore a cloudcap. This was promising, for up there on the top of the mountain sat Zeus, the cloud-gatherer, the thrower of the thunderbolt, the rain-giver. He was a great god. He had other aspects of which we shall hear later. The roar of the thunder was the sign of his power and presence— sometimes of his anger. He smote the high mountains, the tall oaks, and occasionally man with his thunderbolt. But the flash of the lightning and the roar of the thunder were followed by the rain, which moistened the soil and benefited the crops, the grass, and the fruits.

It was seldom necessary to pray for rain in Greece, for the course of the seasons is much more regular there than in northern Europe. Late autumn and winter bring rain; summer brings drought and heat. On the other hand, the weather is not so regular that certain days of the year could be fixed upon for weather magic. This is the reason why as weather god Zeus had few festivals. Sometimes heat and drought were excessive. Myths have much to tell about these disasters, and it is related that they were sometimes so great that the most extreme of all sacrifices, a human sacrifice, was offered. Two such sacrifices are recorded from historical times, one to Zeus Lykaios and one to Zeus Laphystios.[2] Zeus Lykaios received his name from the high mountain in southwestern Arcadia, Lykaion, on the top of which he had a famous sanctuary. Zeus Laphystios was named after the mountain Laphystion in Boeotia, although his cult belonged to Halos in Thessaly. On Mount Lykaion there was a well called Hagno. When there was need of rain the priest of Zeus went to this well, per-

[2] Herodotus, VII, 197, and Pseudo-Plato, *Minos*, p. 315c; Theophrastus in Porphyrius, *De abstinentia*, II, 27.

formed ceremonies and prayers, and dipped an oak twig into the water. Thereupon a haze arose from the well and condensed into clouds, and soon there was rain all over Arcadia.

Zeus Laphystios is well known from the myth of the Golden Fleece, according to which Phrixos and Helle, who were to be sacrificed because of a drought, saved themselves by riding away on a ram with a golden fleece. Their mother was called Nephele (cloud). At the bottom of this myth is weather magic such as is known to have been practiced at several places in Greece, including Mount Pelion, not far from Halos. At the time of the greatest heat young men girt with fresh ram fleeces went up to the top of this mountain in order to pray to Zeus Akraios for cool weather.[3] From this fleece, Zeus was called Melosios on Naxos,[4] and the fleece, which was used in several rites, for example, in the initiation into the Eleusinian Mysteries, was called Zeus' fleece (*Dios kodion*). It is generally said to have been a means of purification and propitiation, and so it was. But its origin is to be found in the weather magic by which the weather god was propitiated. It had a place at Athens in the cult of Zeus Maimaktes, the stormy Zeus, who gave his name to the stormy winter month of Maimakterion.

We are told that in other places, also, people went to the mountain of Zeus to pray for rain. Ombrios and Hyetios are common epithets of Zeus, and we hear of sanctuaries of Zeus on Olympus and on various other mountaintops, such as the highest mountain of the island of Aegina, where he was called Zeus Panhellenios. In this sanctuary a building was erected

[3] C. Müller, ed., *Fragmenta historicorum Graecorum* (Paris, 1841-73), II, 262.

[4] *Inscriptiones Graecae, consilio et auctoritate Academiae litterarum regiae borussicae editae* (Berlin, 1873-), Vol. XII, Fasc. 5, No. 48; interpretation by A. B. Cook, *Zeus; a Study in Ancient Religion* (Cambridge, 1914-25), I, 164.

to accommodate his visitors. Probably the weather god Zeus ruled from the highest peak in every neighborhood. It is supposed that Hagios Elias, who nowadays has a chapel everywhere on the mountaintops, is his successor.

We follow our peasant on his way. We pass the gardens and cornfields where most of his work was done. We shall return to them later. We follow him to those parts of the countryside which were not subject to the labor of men—the meadows and the pasture grounds, the mountains and the forests. Even in modern Greece there are vast tracts of land which cannot be cultivated, and the extent of such land was greater in antiquity. If our peasant passed a heap of stones, as he was likely to do, he might lay another stone upon it. If a tall stone was erected on top of the heap, he might place before it a bit of his provision as an offering (Fig. 4). He performed this act as a result of custom, without knowing the real reason for it, but he knew that a god was embodied in the stone heap and in the tall stone standing on top of it. He named the god Hermes after the stone heap (*herma*) in which he dwelt, and he called the tall stone a herm. Such heaps were welcome landmarks to the wanderer who sought his way from one place to another through desert tracts, and their god became the protector of wayfarers. And if, by chance, the wayfarer found on the stone heap something, probably an offering, which would be welcome to the poor and hungry, he ascribed this lucky find to the grace of the god and called it a *hermaion*.

Our peasant or his forefathers knew that the stone heaps sometimes covered a dead man and that the stone erected on top was a tombstone. Accordingly, the god who dwelt in the stone heap had relations with the dead. Although the people brought libations and food offerings to the dead in their tombs, they also believed in a common dwelling place of the dead.

Such contradictions are hardly noticed by simple people. This abode of the dead, the dark and gloomy Hades, was somewhere far away beneath the earth. On leaving their earthly home, the souls needed someone to show them the way, and nobody was more appropriate for this function than the protector of wayfarers, who dwelt in the stone heaps. Hermes, the guide of souls, is known not only from literature but also from pictures, in which he is represented with a magic rod in his hand, permitting the souls, small winged human figures, to ascend and sending them down again through the mouth of a large jar (Fig. 3). Such jars were often used for burial purposes.

Perhaps our peasant wanted to look after his stock, which grazed on the meadows and mountain slopes. The god of the stone heaps was concerned with them, too. The story, told in the *Homeric Hymn*, how, when a babe, he stole the oxen of Apollo, is a humorous folk tale invented by herdsmen who did not hesitate to augment their herds by fraud and rejoiced in such profitable tricks. One may think of the Biblical story of Jacob and Laban. To Hermes such stories were no boon, for he became the god of thieves.

On Olympus Hermes was a subordinate god, the messenger of the gods, and we know him chiefly as such. I take no account of later additions to his functions, which made him a god of commerce, of gymnastics, and of rhetoric. He was especially popular in one of the backward provinces of Greece, Arcadia, the land of shepherds. Here, too, the herms were especially popular in cult. Attention has recently been drawn to a series of Arcadian herms, some of which are double or triple and inscribed with the names of various gods in the genitive[5] (Fig. 2). Other gods than Hermes were also em-

---

[5] K. Rhomaios, "Arkadikoi Hermai," *Ephemeris archaiologike,* 1911, pp. 149 ff.

bodied in these stone pillars, a relic of the old stone cult, which has left many traces.

According to Hesiod and the *Homeric Hymn*, Hermes cared for and protected the livestock, but we do not find many evidences of this function in his cult. It fell to other gods. Apollo is called Lykeios, an epithet which surely describes him not as the light god but as the wolf god. And why should not the shepherds have appealed to the great averter of evil for protection against the most dangerous foe of their flocks, the wolf? Pastoral life found expression in another god who was always especially Arcadian, Pan. He came to Athens late—not until the time of the Persian wars. He is represented with the legs and face of a goat; he is as ruttish as the he-goat; he plays the syrinx, as the shepherds do in the lazy hours when the flocks graze peacefully; but he may also cause a sudden panic, when the animals, seized for some unknown reason by fright, rush away headlong.

There are many rivers in Greece, but few of them are large. Most of them are small and precipitous, and many are dry in summer. Water is scarce in Greece, and so the benefits received from the rivers are especially appreciated. In ancient times the rivers were holy. An army did not cross a river without making a sacrifice to it, and Hesiod prescribes that one should not cross a river without saying a prayer and washing one's hands in its water. The aid of the rivers was sought for the fertility not only of the land but also of mankind. After the sixth century B.C., names taken from certain rivers were common, for instance, Kephisodotos, the gift of Kephisos. When the young man cut his long hair, he dedicated the locks to the neighboring river.

The rivers each had their god. These gods are represented in the shape of a bull or a bull with a human head (Fig. 6). Such a figure is sometimes called by the name of the great river in northwestern Greece, Acheloos, and Acheloos was venerated in several places in Greece. It is not clear whether the god of the river Acheloos was on his way to becoming a common river god or whether Acheloos is an old word for water. At all events, as the rivers were individualized, so too were their gods.

River spirits in the shape of a bull are well known from European folklore of the present day, and they are certainly an ancient heritage. The river spirit appears just as often, however, in the shape of a horse. This is true, for example, in Sweden and in Scotland. One of the great gods, Poseidon, is closely connected with the horse as well as with water. It is related in some myths that he appeared in the shape of a horse and that he created the horse. He brought forth a spring on the Acropolis of Athens with a stroke of his trident, and Pegasus brought forth the spring of Hippocrene on Mount Helicon with a stroke of his hoof. Other springs, such as Aganippe, also have names referring to the horse. No doubt the water spirit appeared in the shape of a horse also, but the springs had other deities who carried the day, the nymphs, to whom we shall come presently.

To the seafaring Ionians, Poseidon was the god of the sea. On the mainland of Greece, and especially in the Peloponnesus, he was the god of horses and of earthquakes. Earthquakes occur in Greece not infrequently, and when the earth began to tremble, the Spartans used to sing a paean to Poseidon. There is a certain connection between the rivers and the earthquakes, for many rivers in Greece sink down into the ground, eroding the limestone, and flow in subterranean channels for long distances until they break forth again in a mighty stream. The nature philosophers took over from the people the opinion that the earthquakes were caused by this eroding of the ground by the rivers. It is understandable, therefore, that the god of water was also the god of earthquakes. One of the epithets by which he was designated in Laconia, Gaiaochos, has been interpreted as "he who drives beneath the earth."

The Greeks also knew other horse-shaped daemons, the centaurs and the seilenoi. The centaurs have in part the body of a horse and in part that of a man. Homer calls them beasts. They appear only in the myths of art and literature, and they seem to have been localized in two districts, Mount Pelion and northwestern Arcadia. There is no doubt that they were derived from popular belief. If the proposed etymology, according to which the word means "water whipper,"[6] is correct, they were water spirits. In that case, one might believe that they were originally spirits of the precipitous mountain torrents. At all events, their character is rough and violent. They resemble the spirits of wood and wilderness which appear in the folklore of northern Europe. They represent the fierce and rough aspects of nature. They are depicted as using uprooted fir trees for weapons and as carrying the victims of the chase on a pole.

There is another kind of horse daemon, which is often represented in works of art of Ionian origin. These daemons are distinguished from the centaurs by having the body of a man with the legs and tail of a horse and by being ithyphallic. There has been a lengthy discussion concerning their name. It was proposed to assign to these daemons, which were confined to the Ionian area, the name of seilenoi—we know from inscriptions that they were so called—in distinction from the goatlike satyrs, which were supposed to be Dorian.[7] The at-

---

[6] P. Kretschmer in *Glotta*, X (1920), 50.

[7] There has been a lengthy discussion. I cite only E. Reisch, "Zur Vorgeschichte der attischen Tragödie," *Festschrift Theodor Gomperz dargebracht zum siebzigsten Geburtstage* (Vienna, 1902), pp. 451 ff., and the most recent work, F. Brommer, *Satyroi* (Dissertation, Munich, 1937).

tempt to make such a distinction has failed. Proper names prove that seilenoi were well known in the Peloponnesus also,[8] and their value as testimony is the greater because they prove that the seilenoi belong not only to mythology but also to popular belief. Moreover, there are archaic statuettes from Arcadia showing daemons with a human body and features of goats and other animals (Fig. 5). These goatlike daemons are sometimes called *panes*, and they are certainly akin to Pan. The seilenoi and the satyrs have intercourse with the nymphs, and very often they appear dancing and frolicking with the maenads, for they were made companions of Dionysus. We do not know the exact reason why this came about. It is supposed that they were fertility daemons, just as Dionysus was a vegetation god. As a consequence, they appear only in mythology, not in cult. But it is evident that the Greeks peopled untamed nature, the mountains and the forests, with various daemons which were thought of as having half-animal, half-human shape. This is one of the many similarities between Greek mythology and the popular beliefs of northern Europe, in which similar daemons and spirits are numerous. There can be no doubt that centaurs, seilenoi, and satyrs were created by popular belief, although art and literature appropriated them and they had no cult.

Like the peoples of northern Europe, the Greeks knew not only male but also female spirits of nature, the nymphs. The word signifies simply young women, and, unlike the male daemons, the nymphs are always thought of in purely human shape. They are beautiful and fond of dancing. They are benevolent. But they may also be angry and threatening. If a man goes mad it is said that he has been caught by the nymphs. In ancient Greek mythology, as elsewhere, we find the folk-

[8] F. Solmsen in *Indogermanische Forschungen*, XXX (1912), 1 ff.

tale motif of a man compelling a nymph to become his wife. She bears him children but soon returns to her native element. Thetis was originally a sea nymph whom Peleus won by wrestling with her. She soon abandoned his house and only returned from time to time to look after her son, Achilles. Nymphs are often mothers of mythical heroes.

The nymphs are almost omnipresent. They dwell on the mountains, in the cool caves, in the groves, in the meadows, and by the springs. There are also sea nymphs—the Nereids— and tree nymphs. The nymphs had cults at many places, especially at springs and in caves (Fig. 8). Caves with remains of such cults have been discovered. Most interesting is the cave at Vari on Mount Hymettus.[9] In the fifth century B.C., a poor man of Theraean origin, Archedemos, who styles himself "caught by the nymphs," planted a garden, decorated the cave, and engraved inscriptions on its walls. Still more interesting is a cave which was recently discovered at Pitza in the neighborhood of Corinth.[10] The discovery is famous especially for its well-preserved paintings on wood in Corinthian style. One of these tablets represents a sacrifice to the nymphs, and the other represents women. There are a lot of terracottas representing women—some of whom are pregnant—Pan, satyrs, and various animals. The character of the cult and its connection with the nature daemons and with animals is evident, but, on the other hand, it appears that it was pre-eminently a cult of women and that the women applied to the nymphs for help in childbirth. Such cults are also found in other places. In the so-called prison of Socrates at Athens, where a century ago women brought offerings to the Moirai

[9] *Amer. Journ. of Archaeology*, VII (1903), 263 ff.; the inscriptions in *Inscriptiones Graecae*, Editio minor (Berlin, 1913-), Vol. I, Nos. 778-800.

[10] Summary description in *Archäologischer Anzeiger, Beiblatt zum Jahrbuch des archäologischen Instituts*, 1934, pp. 194 ff., and 1935, pp. 197 ff.

for success in marriage and childbirth,[11] the Moirai may have succeeded the nymphs. The nymphs were very popular in cult. They were beautiful and kind and represented the gentle and benevolent aspects of nature and of almost all its parts. It is quite understandable that they were venerated by women especially. Although the cults of women were not absolutely separated from those of men, men and women went different ways and had different occupations in daily life, as they still do in the Greek countryside. The women had their special concerns centering around marriage and childbirth, and it was only natural that they should apply to divinities of their own sex. The nymphs were to be found everywhere and were supposed to be especially benevolent to those of their own sex.

There is a great goddess who is very similar to the nymphs and who is accompanied by nymphs. She is called Artemis, "Lady of the Wild Things." She haunts the mountains and the meadows; she is connected with the tree cult and with springs and rivers; she protects women in childbirth; and she watches over little children. Girls brought offerings to her before their marriage. Her aspect is different in different parts of Greece, but it always goes back to the general characteristics just mentioned, except that one or another of them comes more into the foreground. Her habitual appearance is determined by Homer and the great art and literature of Attica. She is the virgin twin sister of Apollo and by preference the goddess of hunting. How her relation to Apollo came about is not clear. We may only remark here that both carry the bow as their weapon. Of course, the goddess who haunts the mountains and the forests with a bow in her hand is a hunting goddess. Artemis was much more than that, but the Homeric knights, as well as the inhabitants of the great Ionian cities,

[11] J. C. Lawson, *Modern Greek Folklore and Ancient Greek Religion; a Study in Survivals* (Cambridge, 1910), p. 121.

had no relation to the free life of nature except in the sport of hunting, which they loved. Hence, this side of Artemis' nature was especially emphasized.

Other very interesting and very popular aspects of Artemis' nature were prominent, especially in the Peloponnesus. She was closely connected with the tree cult. She is sometimes called Lygodesma, because her image was wound round with willow; Caryatis, after the chestnut; and Cedreatis, after the cedar. Dances and masquerades of a very free and even lascivious character assumed a prominent place in many of her cults, in which men as well as women took part. Cymbals have been found in the temple of Artemis Limnatis in the borderland between Laconia and Messenia.[12] During the excavations of the British School in the famous sanctuary of Artemis Orthia at Sparta, a number of terracotta masks, representing grotesque faces of both men and women, were found (Fig. 7). It is very probable that similar masks were worn by the dancers who performed in this cult. In these customs we find the popular background for the mythological Artemis who dances with her nymphs.

Artemis was the most popular goddess of Greece. She was the leader of the nymphs, and, in fact, she herself was but the foremost of the nymphs. Archedemos, who decorated the cave of Vari, dedicated his inscriptions to the nymphs, but one of them is addressed to the Nymph, in the singular. One of the crowd of nymphs was singled out as a representative of them all, and she became the great goddess Artemis.

Christianity easily swept away the great gods, but the minor daemons of popular belief offered a stubborn resistance. They were nearer the living rock. The Greek peasant of today still believes in the nymphs, though he gives them all the old name

---

[12] H. Roehl, ed., *Inscriptiones Graecae antiquissimae praeter Atticas in Attica repertas* (Berlin, 1882), Nos. 50, 61, 73.

of the sea nymphs, *Neraids.* They haunt the same places, they have the same appearance and the same occupations, and the same tales are told of them. It is remarkable that they have a queen, called "the Great Lady," "the Fair Lady," or even "the Queen of the Mountains." Perhaps she is a last remembrance of the great goddess Artemis, or perhaps there has been a recurrence of the process by which Artemis, the foremost of the nymphs, became a great goddess. Nobody knows, but the fact that the nymphs alone survive in modern popular belief is a telling argument for their popularity among the Greek people in ancient times.

What interests primitive man is not nature in itself but nature so far as it intervenes in human life and forms a necessary and obvious basis for it. In the foreground are the needs of man together with nature as a means of satisfying those needs, for upon the generosity of nature depends whether men shall starve or live in abundance. Therefore, in a scantily watered land such as Greece, the groves and meadows where the water produces a rich vegetation are the dwelling places of the nature spirits, and so are the forests and mountains where the wild beasts live. In the forests the nymphs dance; centaurs, satyrs, and seilenoi roam about; and Pan protects the herds, though he may also drive them away in a panic. The life of nature becomes centered in Artemis, who loves hills and groves and well-watered places and promotes that natural fertility which does not depend upon the efforts of man.

Anyone who wishes to understand the religion of antiquity should have before him a living picture of the ancient landscape as it is represented in certain Pompeian frescoes[13] (Fig. 9) and in Strabo's description of the lowland at the mouth of

---

[13] M. Rostovtzeff, "Die hellenistisch-römische Architekturlandschaft," *Römische Mitteilungen,* XXVI (1911), 1 ff.

the river Alpheus.[14] "The whole tract," Strabo says, "is full of shrines of Artemis, Aphrodite, and the nymphs, in flowery groves, due mainly to the abundance of water; there are numerous hermae on the roads and shrines of Poseidon on the headlands by the sea." One could hardly have taken a step out of doors without meeting a little shrine, a sacred enclosure, an image, a sacred stone, or a sacred tree. Nymphs lived in every cave and fountain. This was the most persistent, though not the highest, form of Greek religion. It outlived the fall of the great gods.

This is not the end of the story. Our peasant certainly passed on his way other small sanctuaries or groves where he paid his respects. Not gods or nature daemons but heroes dwelt in them[15] (Fig. 10). Although modern scholars have proffered other opinions, the Greeks were persuaded that a hero was a man who had once lived, who died and was buried, and who lay in his grave at the place where he was venerated. I should think it likely that our peasant had heard weird stories about heroes, such as those about the hero of Temesa, to whom the most beautiful virgin of the town had to be sacrificed until the famous boxer Euthymus drove him out in a regular fight, or about the hero Orestes, whom the Athenians did not like to meet at night because he was apt to give them a beating and to tear off their clothes. If our peasant became sick he believed, perhaps, that some hero had attacked him. In other words, ghost stories such as are not yet forgotten were told of the heroes. The hero was a dead man who walked about corporeally, a revenant such as popular belief tells of everywhere. But this aspect of the heroes lingered only in the background, for in Greece the heroes had cults and were generally

---

[14] Strabo, VIII, p. 343.

[15] The most comprehensive treatment is by L. R. Farnell, *Greek Hero Cults and Ideas of Immortality* (Oxford, 1921).

helpful. Their cult was bound to their tomb, and their power was bound to their relics, which were buried in the tomb. This is the reason why their bones were sometimes dug up and transferred to another place. Cimon, for example, fetched the bones of Theseus from the island of Scyros to Athens, and the Lacedaemonians with some difficulty found the bones of Orestes beneath a smithy at Tegea and transferred them to Sparta when they wanted his help in the war against the Arcadians. The heroes were especially helpful in war. The sense which the word "hero" had in Homer, namely "warrior," was not forgotten either, and the heroes were particularly well suited to defend the land in which they were buried. In the battle of Marathon, Theseus rose from the ground to fight with his people against the Persians. The Locrians in Italy left a place open in the file for Aias, and in the battle of Sagra he was said to have wounded the commander of their foes, the Crotoniates. It sometimes occurred that a people sent its heroes to help another people.

There were an exceedingly large number of hero tombs and sanctuaries all over the countryside. The names of only the best known of these heroes, and especially those with mythological names, are recorded. Very many were anonymous or called only by some such epithet as "the leader." Others were designated simply by the place where their cult was located. This fact emerges, for example, from the sacrificial calendar of the Marathonian tetrapolis,[16] in which we find four couples, each consisting of a hero and a heroine, and in addition to these some other heroes. In the inscription of the Salaminioi,[17] which was discovered recently during the American excavations at Athens, we also find a series of heroes designated by the localities of their cults in the neighborhood of Sunium.

[16] *Inscriptiones Graecae,* Editio minor, Vols. II-III, Pt. 1, No. 1358.
[17] Published by W. Ferguson in *Hesperia,* VII (1938), 31 ff.

The heroes were exceedingly numerous; they were found everywhere; and they were close to the people. They were thought to appear in very concrete form. It is not to be wondered at that the people applied to them for help in all their needs. They were often healers of diseases, like the Mohammedan saints, whose tombs are often hung with patches torn from the clothes of the sick. Asclepius himself was a hero. He ousted many other heroes who were locally venerated as healers of sickness. Thus the heroes were good for almost everything, and this fact explains why minor local gods who were too insignificant to be reckoned as true gods were received among the number of the heroes. This is the reason why some scholars were prone to consider the heroes as debased gods or "special gods." I cannot enter into this complicated problem, which Farnell has treated fully in his book on the hero cults. I have only wished to give a concrete idea of the importance of the cult of the heroes for the Greek people.

The similarity of the heroes to the saints of the Catholic Church is striking and has often been pointed out. The power of the saints, like that of the heroes, is bound to their relics, and just as the relics of the saints are transferred from one place to another, so were those of the heroes. Moreover, the oracle of Delphi prescribed that a hero cult should be devoted to a dead man if it appeared that a supernatural power was attached to his relics, and the pope canonizes a saint for similar reasons. The cult of the heroes corresponded to a popular need which was so strong that it continued to exist in Christian garb.

I have tried to give as well as possible in a limited space a concrete idea of Greek rustic religion as far as it was concerned with the free life of nature and with the heroes. Nature was peopled with spirits, daemons, and gods. They haunted the mountains and the forests. They dwelt in trees and stones, in rivers and wells. Some of them were rough and dreadful, as the wilderness is, while others were gentle and benevolent. Some of them promoted the life of nature and also protected mankind. The great gods are less prominent in this sphere. Zeus holds his place as the god of the weather, the hurler of the thunderbolt, and the sender of rain. Poseidon appears as the god of water and earthquakes. Hermes is really a minor god, the spirit embodied in the stone heaps, who has been introduced into Olympus by Homeric poetry. Artemis is the foremost of the nymphs who has grown into a great goddess. The innumerable heroes are protectors of the soil in which their bones are laid, ready to help their fellow countrymen in all their needs, linked with both the past and the present.

This aspect of Greek religion was certainly not the highest, but it was the most enduring. It was close to the earth, which is the source of all religion and from which even the great gods sprang. The great gods were overthrown and soon forgotten by the people. The nature daemons and the heroes were not so easily dealt with. The nature spirits have lived on in the mind of the people to this day, as they have in other parts of Europe, although they were not acknowledged by the Church, which called them evil daemons, nor by educated people, who regarded them as products of superstition. The cult of the heroes took on a Christian guise and survived in much the same forms, except that the martyrs and the saints succeeded the heroes.

These facts prove that we have here encountered a religion which corresponds to deep-lying ideas and needs of humanity. They also prove the importance of this kind of religion in antiquity. It was a religion of simple and unlettered peasants, but it was the most persistent form of Greek religion.

RURAL CUSTOMS AND FESTIVALS

I HAVE EMPHASIZED STRONGLY THE FACT THAT EXCEPT for a few industrial and commercial centers ancient Greece was a country of peasants and herdsmen and that according to modern notions many of its so-called cities were but large villages. Certain provinces such as Boeotia, Phocis, and Thessaly, not to speak of Messenia, were always agricultural. In other ways also some of them were still very simple and backward in the classical age. Examples are Arcadia, Aetolia, and Acarnania. Except for those cities to which the leading role in Greek history fell, Greece depended on agriculture and on cattle and sheep raising. In early times, before the industrial and commercial development began, this was true of the whole of Greece, and it was then that the foundations of the Greek cults were laid.

I want to stress this fact and certain of its implications once more. Corn, wheat, or barley was always the staple food of the Greeks. The daily portion of food of soldiers, laborers, and slaves was always reckoned as a certain number of pecks of corn. With the bread, some olives, some figs, or a little goat-milk cheese was eaten and a little wine was drunk. The diet of the Greek peasant is the same even today. Meat was not daily or common food. One might slaughter an animal in order to entertain a guest, as Eumaeus did when Odysseus came to his hut, but this was considered as a sacrifice also. Generally speaking, the common people ate meat only at the sacrifices which accompanied the great festivals. One is reminded of the great feasting on mutton at Easter in modern Greece, where the peasants seldom eat meat. It will be well to keep this background of Greek life in mind when we try to expound the rural customs of ancient Greece.

The significance of agriculture in the popular festivals occurred even to the ancients. Aristotle says that in early times sacrifices and assemblies took place especially after the harvest had been gathered because people had most leisure at this time.[1] A late author, Maximus of Tyre, writes on this topic at greater length.[2] Only the peasants seem, he says, to have instituted festivals and initiations; they are the first who instituted dancing choruses for Dionysus at the wine press and initiations for Demeter on the threshing floor. A survey of the Greek festivals with rites which are really important from a religious point of view shows that an astonishing number of them are agricultural. The importance of agriculture in the life of the people in ancient times is reflected even in the religious rites.

The significance of agriculture in the festivals founded on religious rites goes still further. The Greek calendar is a calendar of festivals promulgated under the protection of Apollo at Delphi in order that the rites due to the gods might be celebrated at the right times. But long before Apollo had appropriated the Delphic oracle for himself, agriculture had created a natural calendar. Agricultural tasks succeed each other in due order because they are bound up with the seasons, and so also do the rites and ceremonies which are connected with these tasks of sowing, reaping, threshing, gardening, and fruit gathering. For all of them divine protection is required

[1] *Ethica Nicomachea,* VIII, p. 1160a.
[2] *Dissertationes,* 30.

and is afforded by certain rites which belong, generally speaking, to an old religious stratum and which have a magical character. Such customs, very similar to those of the Greeks, have been preserved by the European peasantry down to our own day.

The Greek goddess of agriculture was Demeter, together with her daughter Kore, the Maiden. The meaning of -*meter* is "mother." In regard to the first syllable, *de-,* philologists are at variance as to whether it means "earth" or "corn." The cult proves that Demeter is the Corn Mother and her daughter the Corn Maiden. Demeter is not a goddess of vegetation in general but of the cultivation of cereals specifically. The Homeric knights did not care much for this goddess of the peasants. The references to her in Homer are few, but they are sufficient to show that she was the corn goddess who presided at the winnowing of the corn. Hesiod, who was himself a peasant and composed a poem for peasants, mentions her often. For instance, he prescribes a prayer to Demeter and Zeus in the earth that the fruit of Demeter may be full and heavy when the handle of the plow is grasped in order to begin the sowing, and he calls sowing, plowing, harvesting, and the other agricultural labors the works of Demeter.

Agricultural labors were accompanied by rites and festivals, most of which were devoted to Demeter. At the autumn sowing the Thesmophoria was celebrated; in the winter, during which the crops grow and thrive in Greece, sacrifices were brought to Demeter Chloe (the verdure); and when the corn was threshed the Thalysia was celebrated. Best known is the festival of the autumn sowing, the Thesmophoria. There is no other festival for which we have so many testimonies from various places. Demeter herself was called *thesmophoros*, and she and her daughter were the two *thesmophoroi*. The epithet has been translated *legifera*. In this interpretation *thesmos* is taken in the sense of "law" or "ordinance" and reference is made to the conception of agriculture as the foundation of a civilized life and of obedience to the laws. This idea comes to the fore in the Eleusinian Mysteries, which were originally a festival of the autumn sowing like the Thesmophoria to which they were closely akin.[3] It is said that the gift of Demeter is the reason why men do not live like wild beasts, and Athens is praised as the cradle of agriculture and of civilization.

But this interpretation of the word is late and erroneous. It arose only after men had begun to reflect and had recognized that agriculture is the foundation of a civilized life. Thesmos signifies simply "something that has been laid down," and in compound names of festivals ending in -phoria the first part of the compound refers to something carried in the festival. Oschophoria, for example, means the carrying of branches. The thesmoi, consequently, were things carried in the rites of the Thesmophoria, and we know what these things were. At a certain time of the year, perhaps at another festival of Demeter and Kore, the Skirophoria, which was celebrated at the time of threshing, pigs were thrown into subterranean caves together with other fertility charms. At the Thesmophoria the putrefied remains were brought, mixed with the seed corn, and laid on the altars. This is a very simple and old-fashioned fertility magic known from Athens as well as from other places in Greece. The swine was the holy animal of Demeter.

The Thesmophoria and some other festivals of Demeter were celebrated by women alone; men were excluded. Some scholars have thought that the reason for this was that the Thesmophoria had come down from very ancient times when the cultivation of plants was in the hands of the women. This can hardly be so, for the cultivation of cereals with the help

[3] See Chapter III.

of the plow drawn by oxen has always been the concern of men. The Thesmophoria was a fertility festival in which the women prayed for fertility not only for the fields but also for themselves. The parallelism of sowing and begetting is constant in the Greek language. The reason why this festival was celebrated by women alone may simply be that the women seemed especially fit for performing fertility magic.

While the festival of the autumn sowing is very often mentioned, references to the corresponding festival of the harvest, the Thalysia, are curiously few. It is, however, the only festival mentioned in Homer, who says that sacrifices were offered on the threshing floor. Theocritus describes it in his lovely seventh idyl, in the last lines of which he mentions the altar of Demeter of the threshing floor and prays that he may once again thrust his winnowing shovel into her corn heap and that she may stand there smiling with sheaves and poppies in both hands. In modern Europe the harvest home is a very popular rustic festival. The contrast between the popularity of the modern harvest home and the few references to the ancient harvest festival of the Thalysia is probably only seeming. The rites of the autumn sowing, having become a state festival, were celebrated on certain days of the calendar, while the harvest home was in Greece a private festival celebrated on every farm when the threshing was ended and its date was not fixed. It may be added that the harvest is conducted differently in Greece than in northern Europe. The sheaves are not stored in a barn but are brought immediately to the threshing floor and threshed. The harvest in the coast districts falls in May and the threshing at the beginning of June in the dry season when rain is not to be expected. Another harvest festival was probably the Kalamaia, which was not uncommon, though very little is known about it. Its name, derived from *kalamos* (stalk of wheat), its time—June—and its connection with Demeter seem to prove its harvest character.

As becomes a harvest festival, first fruits were offered at the Thalysia. A loaf baked of the new corn was called *thalysion arton*. These loaves are also mentioned in other connections, and Demeter herself received the name of the "goddess with the great loaves." In Attica such a loaf was called *thargelos*, and it gave its name to another well-known festival, the Thargelia. This festival, however, belongs to Apollo, not to Demeter. Its characteristic rite is quite peculiar, and its meaning is much discussed. A man, generally a criminal, was led around through the streets, fed, flogged with green branches, and finally expelled or killed. He was called *pharmakos*, which is the masculine form of *pharmakon* (medicine). Some scholars regard the pharmakos as a scapegoat on whom the sins and the impurity of the people were loaded and who was then expelled or destroyed. They are certainly right. Others have thought that he was a vegetation spirit which was expelled in order to be replaced by a new one. This opinion, too, is not quite unfounded, for fertility magic is conspicuous in the rites. A crossing of various rites has taken place, as happens not infrequently.[4]

The purificatory character of the central rite of the Thargelia explains why the festival was dedicated to Apollo, who is the god of purifications. Purificatory rites are needed and often performed when the crops are ripening in order to protect them against evil influences, and this was probably the original purpose of leading around the pharmakos. References to similar magical rites abound in the writings about agriculture by later authors and are found elsewhere as well. Theo-

---

[4] A survey of the discussion is in my *Griechische Feste von religiöser Bedeutung, mit Ausschluss der attischen* (Leipzig, 1906), pp. 106 ff. See also L. Deubner, *Attische Feste* (Berlin, 1932), pp. 179 ff.

retically, two different kinds of rites can be distinguished, though they are often mixed up. One consists in walking about with some magical object in order that its influence may be spread over the area. The other is encirclement.[5] Conducting the pharmakos through the streets of the town belongs to the former class. So does a kind of magic prescribed for destroying vermin, which required that a nude virgin or a menstruating woman should walk about in the fields or gardens. In the other case, a magic circle is drawn which excludes the evil. It is related of Methana that when winds threatened to destroy the vines, two men cut a cock into two pieces and, each taking a bleeding piece, ran around the vineyard in opposite directions until they met. Thus the magic circle was closed. Magic of a corresponding kind is still practiced in modern times. The leading around of the pharmakos is probably an old agrarian rite which was introduced into the towns and extended to the expelling of all kinds of evil.

Thus, a connection can be established between the chief rite of the Thargelia and the agrarian character of the festival, which is proved by the derivation of its name from thargelos, the loaf offered as first fruit. This presents a certain difficulty, because the Thargelia was celebrated on the seventh day of the month Thargelion, a date which commonly falls a little before harvest time. But it is not without precedent to use unripe ears for the first fruits. The vestal virgins at Rome did so in preparing the *mola salsa* at the commencement of May.

First fruits are commonly considered as a thank offering to the gods, and many people may have brought them with this intention. But like most of the rites and customs discussed here, the offering of first fruits is pre-deistic and older than

[5] See my paper, "Die griechischen Prozessionstypen," *Jahrbuch des Deutschen archäol. Instituts,* XXXI (1916), 319 ff.

the cult of the gods. Its origin is to be found in magic. Among many primitive peoples certain plants and small animals are tabooed during a particular time, and the lifting of the taboo so that they can be used for food is effected by elaborate ceremonies, which are also intended to bring about an increase of these plants and animals. Some scholars are of the opinion that among the Greeks, too, the offering of first fruits and the ceremonial drinking of new wine, of which I shall speak later, represented the breaking of the taboo imposed upon the unripe cereals and wine.[6] Perhaps they are right in regard to the ancient times, about which we have no direct information. The information which has come down to us from the Greeks proves that they themselves thought that the aim of the offering of first fruits was the promotion of fertility. The loaf called thargelos was also called *eueteria* (a good year). It is said, furthermore, that *thargela* were fruits of all kinds which were cooked in a pot and carried around as offerings of first fruits to the gods. The loaf and the mixture of fruit cooked together belong to two different forms of the same custom, to which many parallels are found among modern European peoples, especially in the harvest customs of eating ceremonially some part of the harvest. We have found this custom in the harvest festival of the Thalysia and in the Thargelia, which was celebrated a little before the harvest. It also occurs in the Pyanopsia, which received its name from the cooking of beans in a pot. The Pyanopsia was celebrated in the month of Pyanopsion in late autumn and was a festival of fruit gathering. The *eiresione* (the May bough), about which we shall have something to say later, was also carried

[6] See E. Gjerstad, "Tod und Leben," *Archiv für Religionswissenschaft,* XXVI (1928), 182; for another opinion see J. E. Harrison, *Themis; a Study of the Social Origins of Greek Religion,* 2d ed., rev. (Cambridge, 1927), pp. 291 ff.

around at this festival. The Pyanopsia, as the festival of the fruit harvest, corresponds to the Thalysia, the festival of the cereal harvest.

The meaning of such offerings appears very clearly in an ancient Sicilian custom, which was recorded by ancient students of literature because they believed that they had found in it the origin of bucolic poetry.[7] The so-called bucoliasts went around to people's doors. The goddess with whom the custom came to be associated was Artemis, but the practices which characterize it prove that it belongs among those which we are describing. The bucoliasts wore hartshorns on their heads and carried loaves stamped with figures of animals (this was a concession to the goddess with whom the custom was associated), a sack of fruit of all kinds, and a skin of wine. They strewed the fruit on the thresholds of the houses, offered a drink of wine to the inhabitants, and sang a simple song: "Take the good luck, take the health-bread which we bring from the goddess." What they carried may, in fact, be called a *panspermia*, and the partaking of it conferred luck on the inhabitants of the houses. Similar customs were fairly common. A newly acquired slave and the bridegroom at a wedding were strewn with fruit (*katachysmata*).[8] The custom of strewing the bridegroom with fruit still persists, but its original sense of conferring fertility is forgotten.

This kind of offering is commonly called panspermia, although the Greeks also called it *pankarpia*. Both words signify a mixture of all kinds of fruit. Such offerings were also brought to the dead at the ancient Greek equivalent of All

[7] The passages in question are collected in the introduction to *Scholia in Theocritum vetera*, ed. C. Wendel (Leipzig, 1914), and discussed in my *Griechische Feste*, pp. 199 ff.

[8] Exhaustively treated by E. Samter, *Familienfeste der Griechen und Römer* (Berlin, 1901), but with an interpretation of the custom with which I cannot agree.

Souls' Day, the Chytroi, on the third day of the Anthesteria. It is very interesting that this usage seems to have persisted probably from prehistoric down to modern times. We are told of a vessel, called *kernos*, with many small cups which were filled with fruit of various kinds and with fluids such as wine and oil. In the middle was a lamp. The women carried the kernos on their heads in the Eleusinian Mysteries. Very similar is the *liknon* or winnowing basket filled with fruit, among which a phallus was fixed. It appears in the representations of the Dionysiac Mysteries and is only another way of presenting offerings of the same kind. Vessels of the same shape as the kernos have been found in Minoan Crete and elsewhere, and the conclusion seems to be justified that offerings of this kind were made in the prehistoric age (Fig. 11). The custom has been taken over by the Greek Church. The panspermia is offered to the dead on the modern Greek All Souls' Day, the Psychosabbaton, which is celebrated in the churchyards before Lent or before Whitsunday. It is offered as first fruits on various occasions, but especially at the harvest and at the gathering of the fruit. It is brought to the church, blessed by the priest, and eaten in part, at least, by the celebrants. This modern panspermia varies according to the seasons and consists of grapes, loaves, corn, wine, and oil. Candles are fixed in the loaves, and there are candlesticks with cups for corn, wine, and oil, which have been compared to the ancient kernos.[9] The usual modern name of these offerings is *kollyba*, which signified in late antiquity as well as in modern times an offering of cooked wheat and fruit. The word appears also in descriptions of ecclesiastical usages from the Middle Ages.[10] Very seldom can the continuity of a cult usage be followed

[9] S. Xanthoudides, "Cretan Kernoi," *Annual of the British School at Athens*, XII (1905-6), 9 ff.

[10] Aristophanes, *Plutus*, vs. 678 and scholia. Cf. Hesychius: κόλλυβα. τρωγάλια.

through the ages as this one can. These popular customs, which belong to the oldest and, as some may say, the lowest stratum of religion, are the most long-lived of all.

Up to this point we have dealt chiefly with customs and usages connected with the cultivation of cereals, although in the later paragraphs we have mentioned also some customs pertaining to fruit gathering. As I have remarked, fruit was an important part of the daily food of the Greeks, although we must keep in mind that certain kinds familiar to us, such as oranges, were introduced in recent times. Of wine I need not speak. The cultivation of the olive was very important. Olives were not only eaten as a condiment with bread but also provided the fat which man needs. The oil served for illumination and as a cosmetic. But no special customs referring to the cultivation of the olive are recorded. We know only that at Athens it was protected by Zeus and Athena and that there were sacred olive trees from which came the oil distributed as prizes at the Panathenaean games.

Starting from the beginning of the year, we find a festival celebrated at Athens about the commencement of January. Our information about it and even its name seem to be contradictory. The name, Haloa,[11] is derived from *halos*, which means both threshing floor and garden. Since the first sense of the word would be inapplicable to a festival celebrated in January, it must have been a gardening festival. It is said to have comprised Mysteries of Demeter, Kore, and Dionysus and to have been celebrated by the women on the occasion of the pruning of the vines and the tasting of the wine. It bore a certain resemblance to the Thesmophoria, and sexual symbols were conspicuous in it. If we think of the labors in the vineyards of modern Greece, this account is intelligible though not quite correct. In December the soil is hoed around the

[11] Deubner, *Attische Feste,* pp. 60 ff.

vines, and their roots are cut. At the same time the first fermentation of the wine is ended, and the wine can be drunk, although it is not very good. Thus, the description of the Haloa fits in with what we know about the labors in the vineyards. On the other hand, the Haloa is also said to have been a festival of Demeter, and this, too, is possible. The crops grow and thrive during the winter, and, as we have seen, sacrifices were brought to Demeter Chloe at this time.

In February the vines are pruned, and the second fermentation of the wine comes to an end. The wine is now ripe for drinking. One of the most popular and most complex of the festivals at Athens, the Anthesteria, fell in this season, when spring had come with plenty of flowers. The name means "festival of flowers." We hear of festivals celebrated in other parts of Greece at the season when the vines were pruned. The Aiora, or swinging festival, of the Attic countryside seems to have been of this nature. It was connected with the myth of Icarius, who taught the culture of the vine, and with the Anthesteria. It was a rustic merrymaking. Youths leaped on skin sacks filled with wine, and the girls were swung in swings, a custom which is common in rustic festivals and may perhaps be interpreted as a fertility charm[12] (Fig. 12).

In the city of Athens the most prominent part of the Anthesteria was the blessing and ceremonial drinking of the new wine. The first day, called Pithoigia, had its name from the opening of the wine jars. In Boeotia a similar custom was observed at about the same time, but it was devoted to Agathos Daimon, the god to whom the libation after every meal was made. At Athens the wine was brought to the sanctuary of Dionysus in the Marshes, mixed by the priestesses, and blessed before the god. Everyone took his portion in a small jug, and

[12] See my paper, "Die Anthesterien und die Aiora," *Eranos,* XV (1916), 187 ff.

hence this day is called "the Festival of the Jugs" (Choes). Even the small children got their share and received small gifts, particularly little painted jugs. The schools had a vacation, and the teachers received their meager fee. The admission to this festival at the age of about four years was a token that a child was no longer a mere baby. Another rite pertaining to the Anthesteria was the ceremonial wedding between Dionysus and the wife of the highest sacral official of Athens, the king archon. This is an instance of a widespread rite intended to promote fertility. Examples abound in the folklore of other countries. In Greece they are mostly mythical. At Athens the god was driven into the city in a ship set on wheels (Fig. 13). He was the god of spring coming from the sea.

It is impossible to enter here into a discussion of the very complex rites comprised in the Anthesteria.[13] It should be remarked, however, that the third day, or, more correctly, the evening before it, was gloomy. It was the Athenian All Souls' Day. Offerings of vegetables were brought to the dead, and libations of water were poured out to them. The Anthesteria has a curious resemblance to the popular celebration of Christmas in the Scandinavian countries. Many of the customs observed there at Christmas evidently refer to fertility. People eat and drink heartily and there is much merrymaking. But there is also a gloomy side to the celebration. The dead visit their old houses, where beds and food are prepared for them. There is of course no connection between this festival and the Anthesteria, but only a curious similarity. The popular customs of all countries and of all ages are related.

Vintage festivals are rare in classical Greece. There was one at Athens, the Oschophoria, which got its name from the

---

[13] Deubner, *Attische Feste,* pp. 93 ff. Deubner erroneously denies that the mixing of the wine depicted on certain vases took place at this festival. See my paper, "Die griechischen Prozessionstypen," referred to in note 5 of this chapter.

vine branches laden with grapes which were carried by two youths from the sanctuary of Dionysus to the temple of Athena Skiras. A race followed, and the victor received for a prize a drink made up of five ingredients. At Sparta there was a race of youths, called *staphylodromoi* (grape-runners), at the great festival of the Carnea, which was celebrated about the beginning of September. The name proves that the custom had something to do with the vintage. One of the youths put fillets on his head and ran on before the others, pronouncing blessings upon the town. It was a good omen if he was overtaken by the others and a bad omen if he was not. Many speculations concerning this custom have been advanced, but we cannot with certainty say more than that it seems to have been an old vintage custom. The race reminds one of the race at the Oschophoria.

The association of Dionysus with festivals of viticulture is not nearly so constant as that of Demeter with the cultivation of cereals. The reason is not hard to find. Dionysus came to Greece at a fairly late date—a little before the beginning of the historical age. Viticulture is much older in Greece than he, and the rustic customs which have been described here are very ancient, pre-deistic, magical rites which were not associated with a god until a later time, when it seemed that every festival should be dedicated to a god. The connection was not indissoluble. The gods have vanished, but the customs still persist in part. It is the general belief that Dionysus was above all the god of wine (Fig. 14). Already in Hesiod and Homer wine was his gift. He was not the god of wine alone, however, but of vegetation and fertility in general, though not of cereals. The fig also was a gift from him.[14] In the festival of flowers, the Anthesteria, he appeared as the god of spring.

---

[14] He was called συκάτης in Laconia (Hesychius s.v. συκίτης) and, for the same reason, μειλίχιος on Naxos (Athenaeus, III, p. 78c).

This explains why the phallus was his symbol. The phallus was used in other fertility cults, especially in the festivals of Demeter, but it was nowhere so conspicuous as in the cult of Dionysus. It was carried in all Dionysiac processions. The colonies of Athens were required to send phalli to the Great Dionysia. The procession at this festival, during which the great works of the tragic and comic poets were performed, would make a grotesque impression upon us if we were able to see it with its many indecent symbols. Another Dionysiac festival with a phallus procession was the Rustic Dionysia, which is described by Aristophanes. Rural customs of this sort are mentioned also by Plutarch, who complains that these simple and merry festivals have been ousted by the luxurious life of his times. Comedy had its origin in the jokes and funny songs of the carriers of the phalli. Tragedy also originated in the cult of Dionysus—the cult of Dionysus of Eleutherai, a village in the Boeotian borderland. This cult was brought to Athens by Pisistratus. We ought to keep in mind that in this cult Dionysus was called Melanaigis (he with the black goat-skin) and that there was a myth which proves that a combat between "the Light One" and "the Black One" was enacted. Whether this was the same combat between winter and summer which is found in later European folklore, as some scholars think, I dare not say.[15] But it may not be useless to observe that two of the highest achievements of the Greek spirit, the drama and bucolic poetry, had their origin in simple rural customs.

I have mentioned the eiresione, the May bough, which was carried in the festival of the fruit gathering, the Pyanopsia. It is described in a fragment of a popular song as a branch with leaves hung with figs, loaves, and cups of honey, wine,

[15] See my paper, "Der Ursprung der griechischen Tragödie," *Neue Jahrbücher für klass. Altertum,* XXVII (1911), 673 ff.

and oil.[16] So far it is reminiscent of the panspermia, and it is an appropriate symbol for a festival of fruit gathering. It was carried by a boy whose father and mother were both alive, and it was set up before the temple of Apollo or before the doors of private houses. There it remained until it was dry and likely to take fire. We may guess that it was perhaps exchanged for a new one the following year, just as the modern *bouquet de moisson*, a sheaf decorated with flowers and ribbons, is nailed above the door of the barn at harvest time and remains there until it is exchanged for a new one at the next harvest. The eiresione was also carried at the late spring festival of the Thargelia, mentioned above, and on the island of Samos boys went around carrying the eiresione and asking for alms. The biography of Homer falsely attributed to Herodotus has preserved many precious bits of popular poetry, and among them is the song which the boys sang when they carried the eiresione about. "We come," they sang, "to the house of a rich man. Let the doors be opened, for Wealth enters, and with him Joy and Peace. Let the jars always be filled and let a high cap rise in the kneading trough. Let the son of the house marry and the daughter weave a precious web." The procession and song strikingly resemble modern rural customs in which youths go around asking for alms. To adduce only one example out of many, in southern Sweden they carry green branches, which they fasten to the houses, and sing a song like the ancient Greek one containing wishes for good luck and fertility. This is done on the morning of the first of May. We have already met a similar procession, that of the bucoliasts in Sicily, who carried around and distributed a panspermia, wished good luck, and asked for alms. On the Cyclades the women went around singing a hymn to the Hyper-

[16] Plutarch, *Theseus*, 22.

borean virgins and collecting alms for them.[17] It may be supposed that this custom had something to do with the myth of these virgins and the sheaves which were brought from the Hyperboreans to Delos.

On the island of Rhodes the boys carried a swallow around at the commencement of spring. They began by singing: "The swallow has come bringing the good season and good years." They then asked for loaves, wine, cheese, and wheat porridge. If they were not given anything, they ended with threats. Such threats are often a feature in modern customs also.[18] The poet Phoenix of Colophon, who lived in the third century B.C., composed a similar song for boys who carried a crow.[19] Not only has this custom many parallels in modern times, but it can be demonstrated that it has survived in Greece since antiquity. On the first of March the boys make a wooden image of a swallow, which revolves on a pivot and is adorned with flowers. The boys then go from house to house singing a song, of which many variants have been written down, and receiving various gifts in return.[20] The same custom is recorded for the Middle Ages. It does not seem very much like a religious practice, although it has its roots in religious or magical beliefs, but it shows a greater tenacity than any of the lofty religious ideas.

We return to the May bough which is often carried in such processions. The green branch with its newly developed leaves is the symbol of life and of the renewal of life, and there is no doubt that formerly the purpose of bringing in green branches and setting them up was to confer life and good luck.

[17] Herodotus, IV, 35.
[18] Athenaeus, VIII, p. 360b.
[19] Athenaeus, VIII, p. 359e.
[20] See G. F. Abbott, *Macedonian Folklore* (Cambridge, 1903), p. 18. The songs are collected in A. Passow, *Popularia carmina Graeciae recentioris* (Leipzig, 1860), Nos. 291 ff.

The custom persists, but its old significance has long been forgotten. The May bough is only a lovely decoration. Nowadays we find it at all rural festivals and at family festivals. The same custom prevailed in ancient Greece, though the name of the May bough varied. We have found it in several festivals, sometimes hung with fruits, flowers, and fillets like the modern Maypole. Sometimes the ancient May bough was as elaborately decorated as our Maypole. There is a graphic description of such a Maypole which was carried around the city of Thebes.[21] It was a laurel pole decorated with one large and many small balls of copper, purple fillets, and a saffron-colored garb. This Maypole was carried around at a festival of Apollo, with whom also the May bough is connected. I think it likely that the laurel became his holy tree because it was often used for May boughs.

Sometimes the May bough is simply called by the same name as the loaves which bring luck, *hygieia* (health, health-bringer), a name which proves that it was supposed to confer good fortune. In the Mysteries it was called *bacchos*, a name evidently connected with the role of Dionysus as a god of vegetation. Hence, it is customary to call by this name the bundles of branches tied together by fillets which appear in representations of Eleusinian scenes. In my opinion, the thyrsus which was carried by the maenads, a stick with a pine cone on its top and wound round with ivy and fillets, was just a May bough. We also find pine branches and stalks of the narthex plant in the hands of the maenads. In Sparta there was a cult of Artemis Korythalia, in whose honor lascivious dances were performed and to whose temple sucklings were carried. Her epithet is derived from another name of the May bough, *korythale*. It is said to have been the same as the eiresione. It was a laurel branch which was erected before a house when

---

[21] Photius, *Bibliotheca*, ed. Bekker (Berlin, 1824-25), p. 321b.

the boys arrived at the age of ephebes and when the girls married, just as in modern times the May bough is erected before a house for a wedding.

The May bough was carried in numerous processions. I may recall the *thallophoroi*—dignified old men carrying branches —represented on the Parthenon frieze. The suppliant who sought protection carried a branch wound with fillets, the *hiketeria*. Evidently the idea was that this branch made the suppliant sacred and protected him from violence. Finally, the crown of flowers which the Greeks wore at all sacrifices, at banquets, and at symposia and which the citizen who rose to speak in the popular assembly put on his head is another form of the May bough, and like the May bough it confers good luck and divine protection.

It may perhaps seem that I have wandered far from religion and have chiefly discussed folklore. But the distinction which has been made between religion and folklore since Christianity vanquished the pagan religions did not exist in antiquity. Scholars have been very busy discovering survivals of old magical and religious ideas in our rustic customs and beliefs. In ancient Greece such customs and beliefs were part of religion. Greek religion had much higher aspects, but it had not forsaken the simple old forms. They not only persisted among the people of the countryside, but they also found a place in the festivals and in the cults of the great gods.

These beliefs and customs are time honored and belong to the substratum of religion. They have not much to do with the higher aspects of religion, and they are for the most part magical in significance. They seem quite nonreligious in character, and very often they have changed into popular secular customs. This was not difficult in Greece, for, as we shall see later, the sacred and the secular were intermingled in a manner which is sometimes astonishing to us. But however profane these customs and beliefs may seem to be, their tenacity is extraordinary. Similar beliefs and customs occur everywhere in European folklore, and while the old gods and their cults were so completely ousted by a new religion that hardly a trace of them remains, the old rural customs and beliefs survived the change of religion through the Middle Ages to our own day.

THE RELIGION OF ELEUSIS

A CHAPTER ON THE RELIGION OF ELEUSIS IS A NATURAL
sequel to the description of the rural customs and festivals,[1]
for the Eleusinian Mysteries are the highest and finest bloom
of Greek popular religion. Originally the Eleusinian Mysteries
were a festival celebrated at the autumn sowing. This is proved
by the testimony of Plutarch[2] and by their very near kinship
to the Thesmophoria. Although it is acknowledged that the
basis of the Eleusinian Mysteries is an old agrarian cult, this
fact has been pushed into the background by the attempts to
discover the secret rites of the Mysteries. They have been
discussed repeatedly by scholars and laymen, and numerous
hypotheses have been put forward, some of them intelligent,
others fantastic, none of them certain or even probable. Such
a question seems to cast an everlasting spell on mankind, for
mankind wants to know the unknowable. But the silence imposed upon the mystae has been well kept.

We possess a knowledge of certain preliminary rites which
were not so important that it was forbidden to speak of them.
In regard to the central rites belonging to the grade of the
epopteia, our knowledge extends only to the general outlines.
We know that there were things said, things done, and things
shown, but we do not know what these things were, and that

---

[1] For a full presentation of the materials and arguments see my paper,
"Die eleusinischen Gottheiten," *Archiv für Religionswissenschaft,* XXXII
(1935), 79 ff. See also my forthcoming *Geschichte der griechischen Religion*, Vol. I.

[2] Frag. 23.

is the essential point. The rites consisted, not in acts performed by the mystae, as modern scholars would have us believe, but in the seeing by the mystae of something which was shown to them. This is repeated again and again from the *Homeric Hymn to Demeter* onward, and it is proved by the very name of the highest grade, epopteia, but we do not know what it was that was shown. The name of the high priest, *hierophantes,* proves that his chief duty was to show some sacred things. The names of the family from which he was always taken, the Eumolpidae, and of its mythical ancestor, Eumolpos, prove that he was famous for his beautiful voice. He recited or sang something, but what it was we do not know. Words probably accompanied the showing, but the showing, not the words, was the chief and culminating act of the Mysteries. It should be kept well in mind that the highest mystery was something shown and seen. It may be added that the Mysteries were celebrated by night in the light of many torches, which added to their impressiveness.

The silence imposed upon the mystae has, as I said, been well kept. Only Christian authors, who paid no heed to the duty of silence, have given information concerning the central rites of the Mysteries. But their testimony is subject to the gravest doubts. In the first place, what did they know? Had they any firsthand knowledge? Had they themselves been initiated? Clement lived in Alexandria and the others in Asia or Africa. It is much more probable that what they related was only hearsay. Further, are they reliable? We should realize that their writings were polemics against the perversity of the heathens and that in polemics of this kind controversialists are not conscientious about the means they use if only they hit the mark. Ecclesiastical authors certainly did not trouble themselves much about truth and about such questions of fact as whether a given rite belonged to the Eleusinian or to some other Mysteries, if only they could succeed in impressing upon their hearers or readers a sense of the contemptibility of the Mysteries. The hearers and readers knew nothing for certain and were not able to control the suggestions made to them.

Relying upon such unsafe evidence, modern scholars have tried to find out the kernel of the Eleusinian Mysteries. Two lines of thought are prominent in these attempts. One of these starts from the mysteries of late antiquity, whose highest aim was to elevate man above the human sphere into the divine and to assure his redemption by making him a god and so conferring immortality upon him. It is very questionable whether this idea existed at all in early times, when the gulf separating men from gods was regarded as self-evident and impassable. The supposition that it did exist is very popular in modern research, which has busied itself a great deal with the syncretistic religions of late antiquity; but this supposition should not be admitted without reliable evidence, and of such evidence there is none at all. Sex appeal finds a place even in the science of religion. Scholars have suggested that in the Eleusinian Mysteries immortality was conferred upon the mystes by his being made the son of the goddess through touching some sexual symbol. He was born anew of the goddess in a symbolic way.[3] It is true that Christian authors do ascribe sexual symbols to the Eleusinian Mysteries, and it is possible that there were such symbols at Eleusis, as there were, for instance, in the closely related festival of the Thesmophoria. But if such symbols were used at Eleusis, they did not have the significance suggested above but the old one of fertility charms, as in the Thesmophoria and other ceremonies.

Perhaps a remark is needed on the much-discussed formula

[3] A. Dieterich, *Eine Mithrasliturgie* (Leipzig, 1903), p. 125; A. Körte in *Archiv für Religionswissenschaft*, XVIII (1915), 122 ff.; and C. Picard in *Revue de l'histoire des religions*, XCV (1927), 220 ff.

which Clement of Alexandria gives as that of the Eleusinian Mysteries: "I have fasted, I have drunk of the kykeon, I have taken from the chest, and having worked, I have laid down into the basket and from the basket into the chest."[4] The first two of these rites, the fasting and the drinking of the *kykeon*, are known to have been practiced at Eleusis; but this is not true of the other rites, and it is uncertain whether they belong to Eleusis at all. They may be taken from the Mysteries of Demeter at Alexandria.[5] In any case, this formula refers to the preliminary rites performed by the neophyte, not to the highest mystery, the epopteia. It was pronounced by the neophyte in order to show that he had performed the preliminary rites necessary for being admitted to the final initiation. On this evasive formula are founded the hypotheses mentioned, which try to elucidate the kernel of the Mysteries.

Even if we are precluded from knowing the highest and most central rites of the Eleusinian Mysteries, we are not precluded from knowing the Eleusinian religion—the ideas which were at the bottom of the belief of the initiated in the bliss conferred upon them in the Mysteries. We are acquainted with the gods of the Mysteries, and we know something of the impression made by the celebration and of the hopes which it evoked. We have a document concerning the Eleusinian cult which is older and more comprehensive than anything concerning any other Greek cult, namely, the *Homeric Hymn to Demeter* composed in Attica before Eleusis was incorporated into the Athenian state, not later than the end of the seventh century B.C. We know that the basis of the Eleusinian Mysteries was an old agrarian cult celebrated in the middle of the month Boedromion (about October) and

---

[4] *Protrepticus,* ed. O. Stählin (Leipzig, 1905), p. 16, ll. 18-20.
[5] H. G. Pringsheim, *Archäologische Beiträge zur Geschichte des eleusinischen Kults* (Dissertation, Bonn, 1905), p. 49 and note 1 on p. 58.

closely akin to the Thesmophoria, a festival of the autumn sowing celebrated by the women not quite a month later. I need not dwell upon this connection, which is established by internal evidence as well as by direct information.

According to all probability, the Eleusinian cult goes back to the Mycenaean age. In the excavations of recent years a Mycenaean megaron was discovered beneath the mystery hall.[6] This hall is very unlike a Greek temple, which was the house of a god. It was rebuilt several times, but always according to the old plan. It was a square hall, with pillars supporting the roof and with benches carved in the rock on three sides, destined for the great assembly of the mystae. This hall was called *anaktoron* (the royal house). It has been suggested that the name is reminiscent of a time when the mystery assembly took place in the king's house.[7] The family of the Eumolpidae were the successors of the king, and the cult always remained the property of this family, from which the high priest was taken. Originally the Eleusinian Mysteries were a family cult to which the head of the family admitted whom he pleased. This explains why it was a secret cult and why not only citizens but also strangers and slaves had access to the celebration.

After these preliminaries, we turn to the gods of Eleusis. There were two pairs, one comprising the two goddesses Demeter and Kore, or, more properly, the Mother and the Maid; the other, "the God" and "the Goddess." Both pairs are represented on a relief which Lysimachides dedicated at Eleusis in the fourth century B.C.[8] (Fig. 16). The inscription

---

[6] K. Kourouniotes, "Das eleusinische Heiligtum," *Archiv für Religionswissenschaft,* XXXII (1935), 52 ff.; and my *Gesch. der griech. Rel.*, I, 318, Fig. 4, and 319, Fig. 5.

[7] Deubner, *Attische Feste,* p. 90.

[8] *Ephemeris archaiologike,* 1886, Pl. 3; L. R. Farnell, *The Cults of the Greek States* (Oxford, 1896-1909), III, Pl. 1; and my *Gesch. der griech. Rel.*, I, Pl. 39, Fig. 3.

above the heads of the second pair reads: "To the God, to the Goddess." It is said that "the God" and "the Goddess" were anonymous, and reference is made to the rule forbidding mention of the name of a man who had become a hierophant; but this interdiction is an accretion belonging to a late age, which loved to enhance the mystic character of the cult. In the classical age the hierophants were called by their proper names. Very often, when no misunderstanding was possible, the Greeks said only "the God" or "the Goddess" instead of using proper names. Thus, "the God" at Delphi is Apollo, and "the Goddess" at Athens is Athena. "The God" and "the Goddess" at Eleusis were Plouton and Persephone. They are represented, fortunately with their names inscribed, in a similar scene in a vase painting[9] (Fig. 25), in which Plouton holds his constant attribute, the cornucopia. They are also represented on a badly mutilated tablet from Eleusis.[10]

To each of these two pairs a hero was added, and so we get two triads: Demeter, Kore, and Triptolemos; and "the God," "the Goddess," and Eubouleus. They are seen on an Attic relief found at Mondragone near Sinuessa in Italy,[11] with the addition of a seventh figure clad in a Dionysiac costume—boots and fawnskin. He is Iacchos. Iacchos is a personification of the Iacchic cry heard in the great procession which went from Athens to Eleusis in order to celebrate the Mysteries. The gay revels, the merry cries, and the light of the torches in this procession were reminiscent of the festivals of Dionysus, and the name of Iacchos suggested the second name of this god, Bacchos. So Iacchos was represented in the likeness of Dionysus. But he is a later creation, who owes his existence to the procession mentioned; that is to say, he cannot

[9] Farnell, *Cults of the Greek States,* III, Pl. 8a.

[10] *Ephemeris archaiologike,* 1901, Pl. 2; and my *Gesch. der griech. Rel.,* I, Pl. 41, Fig. 1.

[11] *Bulletin de correspondance hellénique,* LV (1931), Pl. 2.

be older than the incorporation of Eleusis into the Athenian
state, and he was created at the earliest in the sixth century
B.C. There is no question of Dionysiac elements in the Eleusinian Mysteries at an early age, but we shall see that from
the late fifth and early fourth centuries B.C., there was a certain mixing up of the Mysteries of Eleusis and the cult of
Dionysus.

The largest of all Eleusinian monuments, the relief dedicated by Lakrateides, priest of "the God," "the Goddess,"
and Eubouleus, in the year 97-96 B.C.,[12] is peculiar. Happily
the names of the chief figures are inscribed, so that it can be
ascertained that both "the God" and Plouton are represented.
The splitting up of this deity into two is due to the late date
of the monument, for in this age the avoidance of proper
names was current in the Mysteries and thus "the God" and
Plouton might appear as two personages. The daughter of
Demeter also was divided into two goddesses, Kore and Persephone. The two are one and the same person, although they
are represented as two different goddesses. In order to understand how this was possible, we must turn to the myth of the
rape of Demeter's daughter by Plouton. It is the central part
of the *Homeric Hymn*, but it was common to all Greeks. The
Maiden was playing with her comrades in a meadow strewn
with flowers when the earth opened and up came the god of
the nether world in his car. Seizing the Maiden, he abducted
her to his subterranean realm.

Here I take the occasion to mention a legend told in later
sources. A herdsman, Eubouleus, was tending his herd of
swine near by when the earth opened. His swine were swal-
lowed up by the chasm and then the earth closed again. This

---

[12] R. Heberdey in *Festschrift für Otto Benndorf zu seinem 60. Geburtstage* (Vienna, 1898), Pl. 4 and pp. 111 ff.; Farnell, *Cults of the Greek
States,* III, Pl. 2; and my *Gesch. der Griech. Rel.,* I, Pl. 40.

is an explanatory legend, invented to account for a sacred custom. At a certain time of the year, perhaps at the festival of the threshing, pigs were thrown into subterranean hollows. The putrefied remains were brought up again at the festival of the autumn sowing—the Thesmophoria—laid on altars, and mixed with the seed corn—a very simple and old-fashioned fertility charm. The swine was the holy animal of Demeter. Pigs were sacrificed by the mystae before their initiation, and figures of swine are found in Demeter's sanctuaries at Eleusis, at Cnidus, and elsewhere. The connection of Eubouleus with the Eleusinian gods shows that this fertility charm belonged to Eleusis also, and it proves that the Eleusinian festival referred to the autumn sowing. The rite is one of the links between the Thesmophoria and the Eleusinian Mysteries, proving that both were agrarian rites whose purpose was to promote the fertility of the corn which was laid down in the earth.

We revert to the myth told in the *Homeric Hymn*. The Mother wandered about, clad in black garments and carrying torches, in search of her daughter. Coming to Eleusis, she sat down at the well of the maidens, or, as some say, at "the laughless stone." At the well Demeter met King Keleos' daughters, who came to fetch water, and followed them to their father's house. Here she sat down on a seat spread with the skin of a ram. She sat in grief and silence until Iambe by her obscene jests contrived to make Demeter smile. She rejected a cup of wine offered to her and ordered a drink of water mixed with barley meal and pennyroyal. This drink is the kykeon. The story refers to the preliminary initiation, which is represented on certain monuments of the Roman age. Among these is a marble vase described by Countess Lovatelli[13] (Fig. 15). To the right, a youth who is to be initiated

[13] Farnell, *Cults of the Greek States,* III, Pl. 15a; and my *Gesch. der griech. Rel.,* I, Pl. 43, Fig. 2. This and kindred monuments are exhaustively treated by G. E. Rizzo in *Römische Mitteilungen,* XXV (1910), 89 ff.

sacrifices a pig. Then we see him seated with veiled head on a seat decked with a ramskin, while a priestess holds a winnowing basket over his head. This agrarian implement is mentioned in several other Mysteries, especially those of Dionysus, though not at Eleusis. It may be an addition, but it goes well with the character of the Eleusinian cult. Finally, we see the mystes playing with the snake of Demeter, behind whom is Kore. I emphasize again that these were preliminary rites, for this is the reason why they could be mentioned and represented. They are the rites mentioned in the formula of Clement—the fasting and the drinking of the kykeon.

In the house of Keleos, Demeter nursed Demophon, the child of the royal pair. She put him into the fire in order to make him immortal, but her intention was frustrated by the frightened mother, who discovered her in the act. This story is based on an old folk-tale motif which has nothing to do with the Eleusinian cult. It is introduced in order to let Demeter reveal herself in her divine shape. King Keleos ordered a temple to be built for her. Demeter sat in her temple in grief. Not a stalk sprouted in the fields; the labor of the plow oxen was vain; men nearly died of hunger. Zeus was compelled to interfere. He ordered Plouton to send Kore back to the upper world; but Plouton had offered a pomegranate seed to her, and, as she had eaten it, she was bound to the nether world. And so Kore was compelled to dwell one third of the year in the nether world. However, she dwells two thirds of the year in the upper world, reunited with her mother.

This last is the essential point. The understanding of the Eleusinian religion depends on the correct understanding of this myth. The fact that the Maiden dwells two thirds of the year in the upper world and one third in the nether world is manifestly connected with vegetation. Demeter is a goddess of vegetation, but not of vegetation in general. Philologists disagree as to whether the syllable *de-* signifies "earth" or "corn." The cult is decisive. Demeter presides at the threshing and at the autumn sowing. She is the Corn Mother. According to Homer and Hesiod, she united herself with Iasion on the thrice-plowed fallow land and bore to him Ploutos, the god of wealth. The *Homeric Hymn* promises that the goddesses will send him to the house of the man whom they love. Under the conditions prevalent in early times, wealth is the store of corn on which men live during the season when the gifts of nature are scarce. Plouton is only a derivative form of the word *ploutos* and means "he who has wealth." Everywhere in the Mediterranean countries the corn is stored in subterranean silos. An inscription orders such silos to be built at Eleusis for storing the tithes of corn which were brought to the goddesses.

For people who live in a northerly country, where the soil is frozen and covered by snow and ice during the winter and where the season during which everything sprouts and is green comprises about two thirds of the year, it is only natural to think that the Corn Maiden is absent during the four winter months and dwells in the upper world during the eight months of vegetation. And, in fact, this is what most people do think. But it is an ill-considered opinion, for it does not take into account the climatic conditions of Greece. In that country the corn is sown in October. The crops sprout immediately, and they grow and thrive during our winter except for the two or three coldest weeks in January, when they come to a standstill for a short time. Snow is extremely rare and soon melts away. The crops ripen and are reaped in May and threshed in June. This description refers to Attica. The climate is of course different in the mountains, but Eleusis is situated in Attica. The cornfields are green and the crops grow and thrive during our winter, and yet we are asked to believe that the

Corn Maiden is absent during this period. There is a period of about four months from the threshing in June to the autumn sowing in October during which the fields are barren and desolate; they are burned by the sun, and not a green stalk is seen on them. Yet we are asked to believe that during these four months the Corn Maiden is present. Obviously she is absent.[14]

Thus, we are enabled to reach a true understanding of the myth of the absence of the Corn Maiden which agrees with the climatic conditions of Greece. In June the crops are threshed, and the corn, which is the wealth of man, is stored in subterranean silos. In Sicily a festival was celebrated at the time of the threshing which was called the Descent of Kore (*Katagoge Kores*). Down in the subterranean silos the Corn Maiden is in the realm of Plouton, the god of wealth. Four months later, when the time of the autumn sowing is approaching, the silos are opened and the seed corn is brought up. This is the *anodos*, the ascent of the Corn Maiden, and on this occasion the Eleusinian Mysteries took place. The seed corn, the corn of the old crop which will soon sprout and produce the new crop, is laid down in the fields. The Corn Maiden is reunited with the Corn Mother, for at this time the old crop and the new meet each other.

Thus, we are able to understand why Plouton, the god of wealth, had become a god of the nether world. His abode was beneath the surface of the earth, in the silos in which the corn was stored. In early times the corn was often stored in great jars set down into the ground, and such jars were often used for burials also. The myth of the abduction of the vegetation goddess seems to be pre-Greek; and so is the name of

[14] This view is contested by K. Kourouniotes in *Deltion archaiologikon*, XV (1934-35), 1 ff., but I cannot find his arguments conclusive. He does not take into account the fact that Demeter is not a goddess of vegetation in general but of cereals.

Persephone, which occurs in curiously varying forms: Phersephassa and Periphone. It was inevitable that those gods who dwelt beneath the earth should be fused with the lords of the underworld, the king and queen of gloomy Hades. The other aspect of the Corn Maiden was the dreary Persephone, as Homer calls her. Her two aspects were so much at variance that it is not in the least astonishing to find her appearing at Eleusis as Kore, the daughter of Demeter, on the one hand, and as Persephone, the wife of Plouton on the other. Probably two old goddesses were fused into one, the pre-Greek queen of the underworld and the Greek Corn Maiden. These diverse aspects referring to life and death were a source of wealth to the Mysteries. The sprouting of the new crop is a symbol of the eternity of life.

There is, however, another ascent of the Corn Maiden, which follows soon after the fetching of the seed corn from the subterranean silos. It is depicted in some vase paintings,[15] of which one on a mixing bowl in the museum at Dresden is the most remarkable (Fig. 17). There we see Pherephatta emerging from the ground, which reaches her knees, while Hermes assists her, and three satyrs—nature daemons—dance around her.[16] The meaning of this ascent of the Corn Maiden is explained by other vase paintings which seem enigmatical. A great female head emerges from the ground and satyrs strike it with large hammers[17] (Fig. 18). The explanation is not doubtful. A large wooden hammer was a common rustic implement; it was used for smashing the clods and smoothing

---

[15] They are enumerated and discussed in an appendix to my paper, "Die eleusinischen Gottheiten," pp. 131 ff., referred to in note 1 of this chapter.

[16] *Archäologischer Anzeiger*, 1892, p. 166; J. E. Harrison, *Prolegomena to the Study of Greek Religion*, 3d ed. (Cambridge, 1922), p. 277, Fig. 67; Farnell, *Cults of the Greek States*, III, Pl. 6b; and my *Gesch. der griech. Rel.*, I, Pl. 39, Fig. 1.

[17] Harrison, *Prolegomena*, p. 279, Fig. 69; and my *Gesch. der griech. Rel.*, I, Pl. 39, Fig. 2.

the surface of the fields, which was very rough after the seed corn was plowed under. This process, which corresponds to the rolling of the present day, was carried out just when the corn had begun to sprout and when it was still possible to walk on the fields without doing harm to the crops. It concurred with the second ascent of the Corn Maiden, the germinating of the new crop.

The reuniting of the Mother and the Maid was the kernel of the myth. Judging from the nature of the festival, it must likewise have been the kernel of the Eleusinian Mysteries, which were a celebration of the ascent of the Corn Maiden in the autumn sowing. The old agrarian myth was elevated into the human sphere. The grief and sorrow of the bereaved mother, the despair of her search, touch upon the deepest feelings of man. Demeter is rightly called the *mater dolorosa* of Greek religion. To this heartbreaking sorrow, the reunion of mother and daughter provided a joyful contrast, rousing the mystae to exultation and moving their minds with the deepest emotions. The Mysteries were not a gloomy festival; they conferred joy and happiness upon man. Not the rape and separation but the reunion was its theme. The reunion is represented on the famous tablet of Ninnion from the end of the fifth century B.C., found in the sacred precinct at Eleusis[18] (Fig. 21). In the lower zone Demeter is seated, and at her side is a vacant seat; Kore is absent. Demeter is approached by Iacchos, the leader of the great procession to Eleusis, and by two mystae. In the upper zone we again see Demeter seated. A stately woman approaches, carrying torches and followed by mystae, a woman with a kernos (a vessel used in the mysteries) on her head, a youth, and a man. It is Kore,

---

[18] *Ephemeris archaiologike,* 1901, Pl. 1; Farnell, *Cults of the Greek States,* III, Pl. 16; and my *Gesch. der griech. Rel.,* I, Pl. 41, Fig. 2.

brought back to her mother. This is, of course, not a direct representation of a scene in the Mysteries, which it was forbidden to divulge not only in words but also in pictures. It is a mythical scene with features borrowed from the mystery procession. We do not know if the reuniting of mother and daughter was enacted in the Mysteries, but it must have been in the minds of all. Perhaps it was enacted in some manner, perhaps it was only indicated symbolically. A Christian writer says that the highest mystery of the epopteia at Eleusis was a reaped ear of corn shown in silence.[19] It may be that this statement is more trustworthy than others, for it agrees exactly with the simple old agrarian character of the Eleusinian cult. In this connection, mention is often made of the picture on an Apulian tomb vase, which shows five ears of corn in a sacellum, very carefully drawn[20] (Fig. 20). Of course it has nothing to do with the Eleusinian Mysteries, but it is an expression of the same belief in the sacredness of the ear of corn, the symbol of the eternity of life. The purpose of these rites at the autumn sowing, that which the celebrants hoped for, was the new crop. Here it was—the ear held up in the hands of the hierophant. All saw that their hopes would be fulfilled; nay, were fulfilled. Here was she who had long been absent and had been sought for in vain, the Corn Maiden, reunited with the Corn Mother. For, if this information is reliable, I should like to call the ear of corn the Corn Maiden.

The old agrarian cult was capable of carrying other ideas of a moral character. We have heard that Triptolemos was added to the pair of goddesses. Originally, this was not so.

[19] Hippolytus, *Refutatio haereseon*, V, 8, 39.

[20] P. Wolters, "Die goldenen Ähren," *Festschrift für James Loeb zum sechzigsten Geburtstag gewidmet* (Munich, 1930), p. 124, Fig. 14; Farnell, *Cults of the Greek States*, III, Pl. 3b; and my *Gesch. der griech. Rel.*, I, Pl. 42, Fig. 3.

In the *Homeric Hymn* he is barely mentioned as one of several Eleusinian noblemen. We are able to trace his rise to a higher dignity. It was due to his name, which may signify the "thrice warring," but which was understood as the "thrice plowing." He became the hero of the thrice-plowed cornfield and is sometimes represented with a plow in his hand[21] (Fig. 23). Pausanias mentions the threshing floor of Triptolemos in the sacred Rharian field near Eleusis, the cradle of agriculture, where corn was sown for the first time. Triptolemos begins to appear in paintings on black-figured vases in the late sixth century B.C., represented as a bearded hero[22] (Fig. 19). In the vase paintings of the early red-figured style he is extremely popular. He is seated on a winged car drawn by serpents and is placed between the two goddesses, who offer him the cup of farewell as they send him out on his mission to propagate agriculture[23] (Fig. 22). Even when other gods are added, Triptolemos is the central figure.

We know the meaning of this scene from the praises bestowed upon Athens as the cradle of civilization. Isocrates speaks in his *Panegyricus* of the two greatest gifts granted the Athenians by Demeter—the corn, which is the reason why men do not live like wild beasts, and the Mysteries, from which they derive higher hopes in regard to their life and all time. The *dadouchos* Kallias said something similar in the peace negotiations at Sparta in 372 B.C. This praise of Athens is behind the decree of 418 B.C., in which the Athenians invited all Greeks to bring tithes to the Eleusinian goddesses

---

[21] *Athenische Mitteilungen,* XXIV (1899), Pl. 7; and Harrison, *Prolegomena,* p. 273, Fig. 65.

[22] W. H. Roscher, *Ausführliches Lexikon der griechischen und römischen Mythologie* (Leipzig, 1884-1937), Vol. V, col. 1127, Fig. 1.

[23] The most beautiful example is a skyphos by Hieron. It is often reproduced. See A. Furtwängler and K. Reichhold, *Griechische Vasenmalerei* (Munich, 1900-1932), Pl. 161; Farnell, *Cults of the Greek States,* III, Pl. 13; and my *Gesch. der griech. Rel.,* I, Pl. 43, Fig. 1 (part).

according to old custom and an oracle from Delphi.[24] At this time Eleusis must have been recognized as the cradle of agriculture.

The vase paintings mentioned show how strongly the benefits of agriculture were felt at the end of the sixth and the beginning of the fifth century B.C. This feeling was of course not limited to the cultivation of cereals, but referred especially to the moral and social consequences of agriculture. I should like to refer to a parallel, the exploits of the Athenian national hero Theseus, which were very popular in vase paintings of the same age. It is said that the Athenians wished to create a counterpart of Heracles for themselves, but a great difference between Heracles and Theseus is to be noted. While the exploits of Heracles are those of an old mythical hero, Theseus conquers highwaymen and robbers who resist civilization and are dangerous to it. Theseus is the guardian and hero of a peaceful and civilized life, of which agriculture is the foundation.

The peasant loved peace. In war his fields were burned and his trees cut down. Hesiod says that for the wild beasts the law is to eat each other, but Zeus has given justice to man. Hesiod preaches labor, through which man earns his livelihood, and justice, which assures him of the fruits of his labor. Hesiod has abandoned the ideal of the warring Homeric knights and embraced a new, quite contrasted ideal of peace and justice created by agriculture. Its hero is the Eleusinian Triptolemos. This is a complete revolution in moral ideals, which ought to be appreciated to its full extent. I venture to speak of an Eleusinian piety founded on this idea that agriculture created a civilized and peaceful life worthy of human

---

[24] Isocrates, *Panegyricus,* 28; Xenophon, *Hellenica,* VI, 3, 6; the decree in W. Dittenberger, *Sylloge inscriptionum Graecarum,* 3d ed. (Leipzig, 1915-24), Vol. I, No. 83.

beings. Aristophanes speaks of it in some remarkable verses of his comedy *The Frogs*.[25] The mystae sing: "The sun and the gay light are only for us who are initiated and live a pious life in regard to foreigners and private persons." In order to attain to the better lot in the other world for which the mystae hoped, it was necessary to have been initiated; but here there is added to this requirement the further requirement of a pious life, specified in a somewhat pedantic manner by the words "in regard to foreigners and private persons." Among the private persons were also the slaves. Slaves as well as foreigners were admitted to the Eleusinian Mysteries, provided that they spoke Greek. In antiquity foreigners and slaves were excluded from the protection of civil law. This traditional limit was transcended in the Mysteries. They could not grant the protection of the law, but they demanded the piety which implies the law and is more than the law. In fact, an effort was made to break the traditional bonds of the local city-state and to attain to the idea of humanity as a great brotherhood. This morality issued from the agricultural conditions prevalent in Attica in the early age and was developed in the old agricultural cult of Eleusis.

The Eleusinian Mysteries had still more to offer to the initiated. The *Homeric Hymn* promises: "Happy is he who has seen this. Who has not taken part in the initiation will not have the same lot after death in the gloomy darkness."[26] Sophocles repeats the same idea in still more impressive words. He says that those who have seen the Mysteries are thrice happy when they go to the underworld, and adds that for them only is life, for others all is evil.[27] Aristophanes in *The Frogs* introduces a chorus of mystae in the scene which is laid in the

[25] *Ranae,* vss. 454 ff.
[26] *Homeric Hymn to Demeter,* vss. 480 ff.
[27] Frag. 753, in A. Nauck, *Tragicorum Graecorum fragmenta,* 2d ed. (Leipzig, 1889).

underworld. I have already quoted his words. The mystae dance and revel in a meadow strewn with flowers. This conviction of a happier lot in the underworld, which filled the minds of the initiated, sprang from ancient roots, the worldwide idea that the other life is a repetition of this life. The idea is found, for example, in the eleventh book of the *Odyssey*, which describes Odysseus' visit to the underworld. The simple fact is that the initiated believed that they would continue to celebrate the Mysteries in the underworld, as Aristophanes and Euripides[28] show them doing. Since the Mysteries were the most edifying event they knew of, such a conception of a future state formed the brightest possible contrast to the dark and gloomy Hades in which the Greeks believed.

This is really a very simple belief, and perhaps it satisfied the great mass. But it may be permitted to ask whether deeper ideas of life and death were not evoked by the Eleusinian Mysteries. Perhaps they were. In a remarkable fragment Pindar says: "Happy is he who, having seen this, goes beneath the earth; he knows the end of life and he knows its god-sent beginning."[29] We do not know if Pindar was initiated, but supposing that his words really refer to Eleusinian beliefs, we will try to interpret them. What is the beginning of life? If we remember that the Mysteries were a festival of the autumn sowing, the ascent of the Corn Maiden, we are reminded of the words in the Gospel of St. John: "Except a corn of wheat fall into the ground and die, it abideth alone: but if it die, it bringeth forth much fruit."[30] It is related that the Athenians sowed corn on graves and that they called the dead *demetreioi*.[31] In a well-known hymn, the Christian poet

[28] Euripides, *Hercules furens,* vs. 613.

[29] Frag. 137, in T. Bergk, *Poetae lyrici Graeci,* 4th ed. (Leipzig, 1878-82).

[30] Gospel of St. John, 12:24.

[31] Cicero, *De legibus,* II, 63, from Demetrius of Phaleron; Plutarch, *De facie in orbe lunae,* p. 943b.

Prudentius uses the same simile for the resurrection of the individual; but we have no right to postulate this idea for an age when conscious individualism was unknown and when the individual was only a link in the chain of the generations. Such an age had no need of a belief in the immortality of the individual, but it believed in the eternity of life in the sense that life flows through the generations which spring from each other. No clearer, no better expression of this belief can be found than the sprouting of the new crop from the old crop which has been laid down in the earth. It is the second ascent of the Corn Maiden, which was familiar to that age from its labors and which was the immediate result of the autumn sowing celebrated in the Eleusinian cult.

The latest monument of art which represents the mission of Triptolemos is the famous Eleusinian relief (Frontispiece), which better than any other conveys an idea of the high artistry and the deep religious feeling of Phidias. Triptolemos is almost a boy standing between the two goddesses. This relief was sculptured about 440 B.C. In later monuments Triptolemos often appears, but only as a member of the assembly of the Eleusinian deities. He is no longer the central figure. To the Eleusinian deities, others are added: the city goddess of Athens; Dionysus, who in this age had a certain connection with Eleusis; and more heroes—Heracles and the Dioscuri. These heroes, the first strangers to be initiated, recall the Panhellenic aspirations of the Eleusinian Mysteries. Such representations are manifestly a product of the interest taken in the Eleusinian Mysteries, but they do not express any special idea, as the representations of Triptolemos and the Ninnion tablet do.

Certain other vase paintings are more interesting because they introduce a novelty. A child appears among the Eleusinian deities. Most remarkable is a hydria found in Rhodes[32] (Fig. 24). A woman has partly emerged from the ground, which reaches to her breast. She holds a cornucopia on which a child is seated. The child stretches out its arms toward a goddess with a scepter, who must be Demeter, for on the other side is Kore with two torches and above her is Triptolemos. A pelike from Kertsch shows a woman rising from the ground and handing over a child to Hermes, at whose side is Athena.[33] To the left are Demeter and Kore, and to the right are "the God" and "the Goddess," that is Plouton and Persephone. On the other side, and on a vase in the collection at Tübingen, the child is a little older. He stands at the side of Demeter and holds a cornucopia.[34]

In these paintings the birth of a child is represented in Eleusinian surroundings. The type is well known from the representations of the birth of Erichthonios, but this Athenian hero has no connection with Eleusis. The cornucopia which the child carries, and on which it is seated in the picture on the hydria from Rhodes, puts us on the right track. The cornucopia is the attribute of the god of wealth, Plouton. The ideal embodied in this god was popular at the time to which these vases belong. The most famous example is the group by Kephisodotos, erected in 372 B.C., in which the goddess of peace carries the child Ploutos in her arms. It is an expression of the hopes of the Athenian people in those troubled times.

[32] It is often reproduced. See Harrison, *Prolegomena,* p. 525, Fig. 151; and my *Gesch. der griech. Rel.,* I, Pl. 44, Fig. 1.

[33] Admirably reproduced in Furtwängler and Reichhold, *Griechische Vasenmalerei,* Pl. 70. See also Farnell, *Cults of the Greek States,* III, Pl. 21a (the side with Hermes); and my *Gesch. der griech. Rel.,* I, Pl. 46.

[34] C. Watzinger, *Griechische Vasen in Tübingen* (Reutlingen, 1924), Pl. 40; and my *Gesch. der griech. Rel.,* I, Pl. 45, Fig. 1. Unfortunately this vase was overlooked in my paper, "Die eleusinischen Gottheiten," referred to in note 1 of this chapter. On the interpretation see my *Gesch. der griech. Rel.,* I, 295, note 4.

In the foregoing we have heard of Plouton as a full-grown god, and he is sometimes represented as a white-haired old man.[35] But we have also mentioned the myth that Demeter bore Ploutos, having united herself with Iasion on the thrice-plowed fallow land. We find representations of Ploutos at all stages of life, corresponding to the cycle of vegetation. Without any doubt, Ploutos is the child who appears in the vase paintings mentioned. Except for these vase paintings, we hear nothing of the child Ploutos at Eleusis. The reason is very simple. By the side of the daughter of Demeter, whose part was most prominent, there was no place for the son of Demeter. He would have been completely out of accord with the idea expressed in the Eleusinian myth. His reappearance in the fourth century B.C. is a kind of atavism, due to the longing of that age for the security of peace and wealth. Kephisodotos called the mother "Peace." For the vase painters, her name was probably Ge (the earth), from which the crops sprout. Ploutos appeared only for a brief time, and he vanished as quickly as he had come, but that he did appear proves that new ideas could find a place in the minds of those who were initiated into the Eleusinian Mysteries.

At the same time, Dionysiac elements were introduced at Eleusis. One connecting link was, of course, Iacchos, whose similarity to Dionysus-Bacchos was pointed out above. But there were also internal connections, for the cult of Dionysus in one of its aspects had to do with the cycle of vegetation. At Delphi he was represented as a child in a winnowing basket, awakened by the maenads. According to Furtwängler, the child which is handed over to Hermes on the pelike from Kertsch is wrapped in a fawnskin and crowned with ivy, and

---

[35] On a Nolan hydria; see British Museum, *Corpus vasorum antiquorum* (London, 1925-), Fasc. 6, Pl. 84, Figs. 2a-c. For Plouton alone see Farnell, *Cults of the Greek States,* III, Pl. 32a.

on a vase from the Hope collection we see Dionysus emerging from the ground like the Corn Maiden.[36] We have seen further that in several late Eleusinian vase paintings Dionysus is introduced among the Eleusinian deities. This is a forerunner of the coalescence between various mystery cults, which became common in a later age. There are traces of this syncretism in the Roman age, with which I cannot deal here.

The rites of the Eleusinian Mysteries were persistently preserved from a hoary antiquity, although they, too, may have been somewhat modified in the course of time. There were no doctrines, however, but only some simple fundamental ideas about life and death as symbolized in the springing up of the new crop from the old. Every age might interpret these according to its own propensities. Thus the persistence of the most venerable religion of ancient Greece is explained. Its power was a result of the absence of dogmas and of its close connection with the deepest longings of the human soul.

So it was possible to develop on the foundation of the old agrarian cult a hope of immortality and a belief in the eternity of life, not for the individual but for the generations which spring one from another. Thus, also, there was developed on the same foundation a morality of peace and good will, which strove to embrace humanity in a brotherhood without respect to state allegiance and civil standing. The hope and the belief and the morality were those of the end of the archaic age. The thoroughly industrialized and commercialized citizens of Athens in its heyday had lost understanding of the old foundation of human civilization—agriculture—and at the end of the fifth century B.C. the individual was freed from the old fetters of family and tradition. The foundations for the idealism of the Eleusinian belief and morality were removed. Man

[36] E. M. W. Tillyard, *The Hope Vases* (Cambridge, 1923), No. 163, Pl. 26, and pp. 97 ff.

was no longer content with the immortality of the generations but wanted immortality for himself. The Eleusinian Mysteries promised even this in a happy life in the underworld. If a man underwent initiation into the Eleusinian Mysteries in this era, he did so because he hoped for a happier life in the other world and because he found the celebration of the Mysteries edifying. The hero of agriculture became only a concomitant figure in the assembly of the Eleusinian gods. Dionysus was added, and the child which brings wealth reappeared. But participation in the mystery rites was still a religious experience, which had the power of conferring happiness on man and of helping him through life. For it was an experience that was rooted in the deepest feelings of man and spoke to his heart, although its language changed with the changing ages.

THE HOUSE AND THE FAMILY

A GREAT SCHOLAR HAS GRAPHICALLY DESCRIBED ARTEMIS as the goddess of the outdoors (Göttin des Draussen). Untamed nature may be lovely and beneficent, but, on the other hand, it may be terrible and frightful. The desert wilderness, the rugged mountains, the deep ravines, the precipitous torrents, and the thick forests inspire awe in man. Among them he feels himself subject to unknown and dangerous powers. There the wild beasts which attack him and his herds roam about, and robbers may lurk in the glens. "It is better at home, for it is dangerous outdoors" is an old Greek saying, found in Hesiod and in the *Homeric Hymn to Hermes*.[1] Within the walls of his house, man feels himself secure, protected from dangers which threaten without. The ancient Greeks would have understood what we mean when we say, "A man's house is his castle." In the beginning of the work of Thucydides there is a vivid description of how unsafe life was in early times because of robbers and pirates.

Descriptions in Homer, supported by archaeological evidence, give us an idea of the house of the early age in its main lines. It was a great, square, single-roomed house—a hall with a porch or forehall on one of its shorter sides and a fixed hearth in its midst. It stood in a courtyard, surrounded by a wall or fence to protect the inhabitants against the attacks of

---

[1] Hesiod, *Opera,* vs. 365, and *Homeric Hymn to Hermes,* vs. 36.

wild beasts and human foes. This house or hall is generally called a *megaron*. It is by its nature an isolated building, standing free, not connected with other houses, and adapted to country life. But already in prehistoric times there were towns in Greece with complex buildings and narrow streets,[2] and in the great palaces of the Mycenaean age the megaron was introduced into a complex building plan. We may confidently suppose that the detached house with its enclosed courtyard survived for a long time in the countryside, but such mean houses were so lightly built that they have left no traces. When people settled together in towns or large villages, lack of space caused a modification of the plan. The houses were built together and connected, the fence disappeared, and the courtyard was reduced; but the characteristic form of the great living room, the megaron, remained, even in the city of Priene, which was built at the time of Alexander the Great.

The house and its fence protected man against enemies and other dangers, but it needed divine protection itself. Its protector was Zeus, whom we here meet in various roles quite different from that of the weather god. The Greek word for fence is *herkos*, and *herkeios* is an epithet of Zeus. According to Homer, the altar of Zeus Herkeios generally stood in the courtyard before the house, where sacrifices and libations were offered to him. Mythology emphasizes the savagery of Neoptolemus by making him slay the aged Priamus on the very altar of Zeus Herkeios. An altar of Zeus Herkeios was to be seen among the ruins of the house of Oinomaos at Olympia. He is found at Sparta as well as at Athens, where Aristophanes and Sophocles mention him. In Sophocles his name is used to designate the whole family. A much more important fact is that at Athens, when the newly elected archons were examined, they

[2] Best known is the town excavated by M. N. Valmin on Malthi and described in his work, *The Swedish Messenia Expedition* (Lund, 1938).

were asked whether they owned an Apollo Patroos and a Zeus Herkeios and where these sanctuaries were, for this question presupposes that every citizen had an altar of Zeus Herkeios. The divine protector of the house was found in every house; but his name proves that originally he was the protector of the fence which surrounded the house and that he guarded it against dangers from without.

There is another rather curious instance of the protection which Zeus afforded to the house. He was the god of lightning, and as such he was named Kataibates[3] (he who descends), that is to say the thunderbolt, which was imagined to be a stone or a stone ax. Stones inscribed with the name of this god have been found. Now an altar dedicated to Zeus Kataibates stood beside that of Zeus Herkeios in the ruins of the house of Oinomaos, another was found in a house on the island of Thera, and at Tarentum there were altars before the houses on which sacrifices were made to Zeus Kataibates. The altars were erected and the offerings were made in order to protect the house from a stroke of lightning. This custom seems to have been fairly common.

Much more important and interesting is another form of Zeus in which he appears as a house god, Zeus Ktesios, the most curious of all, because the sky god appears in the guise of a snake. He is not very often mentioned, for on the whole the simple house cult belonged to the daily routine for which literature cared little. But that he was venerated in all of Greece is proved by the fact that this epithet also appears in the Doric form *Pasios*. It is exceptional for an epithet thus to appear in various dialectic forms. Both Ktesios and Pasios signify "the Acquirer." Sometimes the name is used without the

[3] See my paper, "Zeus Kataibates," *Rheinisches Museum*, XLIII (1908), 315 ff. For the various aspects of Zeus mentioned here see also the great work by A. B. Cook, *Zeus*.

addition of Zeus. An altar of Zeus Ktesios is mentioned by Aeschylus, an altar dedicated to him was found in a house on the island of Thera, and there are other such altars of a small size with his name. On the island of Thasos he is called Zeus Patroos Ktesios,[4] and in its colony Galepsos in Thrace he appears in company with Zeus Herkeios Patroos.[5] He was still not forgotten in the Roman era. Finally, on a relief found at Thespiae his name is inscribed above a great snake (Fig. 26). Fortunately, Attic writers give some information about his cult. Menander says that he was the protector of the storehouse and that his function was to guard this against thieves.[6] It is said that his "image" was erected in the storehouse. Another Attic writer, who treated of the cults, explains the kind of image these were. He calls them *semeia* (tokens or symbols).[7] These were jars or amphorae, the handles of which were decorated with woolen fillets and into which were put fresh water, oil, and fruit of all kinds. The Greek word for this mixture was panspermia or pankarpia, a kind of offering which we have become acquainted with in the agrarian cults. I suppose that this offering was a meal offered to the house god and that the house god in the shape of a snake came to partake of it.

That this supposition is right is proved by a cult that is familiar under quite a different aspect, that of the Dioscuri,[8] the sons of Zeus as their name indicates. I shall not here go into their generally known appearance and cult, but shall confine myself to their role in the house cult. The form in which the Dioscuri appear in mythology and in their cult in later times is certainly the result of a blending of various elements.

[4] *Revue archéologique,* IX (1937), 195.

[5] Dittenberger, *Sylloge inscriptionum Graecarum,* Vol. III, No. 991.

[6] *Pseudo-Herakles,* frag. 519, in T. Kock, *Comicorum Atticorum fragmenta* (Leipzig, 1880-88).

[7] Anticleides, in Athenaeus, XI, p. 473b.

[8] See my book, *The Minoan-Mycenaean Religion and Its Survival in Greek Religion* (Lund, 1927), especially pp. 469 ff.

They were also called *Anaktes* (kings), and sometimes they appear as children. Their cult was especially popular at Sparta, where they were evidently house gods. A series of reliefs shows their symbols and cult paraphernalia. Their special symbol was the *dokana*, two upright beams joined by two transverse beams. This has been interpreted variously and ingeniously both in ancient and modern times. The simple explanation is that the dokana represent the wooden frame of a house built of crude bricks. On certain reliefs from Sparta and from its colony Tarentum, and on Spartan coins, two amphorae appear as the symbols of the Dioscuri (Fig. 29). A snake approaches them or is coiling around them or the beams of the dokana (Fig. 31). That the Dioscuri were house gods is proved by their cult. A meal was set out and a couch prepared for them in the house. This is what Euphorion did;[9] Phormion was punished because he would not open the chamber of his house to them.[10] These meals were called *theoxenia*. Theron of Agrigentum and Iason of Pherae prepared meals in honor of the Dioscuri, and Bacchylides in a poem invites them to a meal from which wine and songs will not be missing. The Athenians spread the table in the prytaneum for them with a frugal, old-fashioned meal of cheese, cakes, olives, and leeks. Some vase paintings and reliefs show the Dioscuri coming to the meal. Here they are riding, in accordance with the common conception (Fig. 32). In Sparta they appear as snakes. The close affinity of Zeus Ktesios and the sons of Zeus is apparent.

Another Zeus, for whose occurrence in the house cult there is no evidence, must be mentioned because he is not infrequently represented as a snake. This is Zeus Meilichios, who was much venerated in Attica (Fig. 27). He is also represented as seated on a throne with a cornucopia (Fig. 28); he is accord-

[9] Herodotus, VI, 127.
[10] Pausanias, III, 16, 3.

ingly akin to Zeus the Acquirer. His name signifies the one who has been propitiated, he is the propitious one. This is probably the reason why he became like Zeus the Acquirer. Zeus Soter, the Savior, also seems to have been connected with Meilichios at Piraeus. I do not speak here of that Zeus Soter whom the cities celebrated as the savior of their political freedom, but of the Zeus Soter of the house cult. To him, some of the altars which were found in the houses of the island of Thera are dedicated. Aeschylus says that besides the upper and nether gods he is the third protector of the house. At the symposium the first and third libations were devoted to him. No representations of him in snake form are known, however. Finally, we must mention Agathos Daimon, the Good Daemon, whose name is inscribed on one of the house altars from Thera. At the end of the daily meal a few drops of unmixed wine were poured out on the floor as a libation to Agathos Daimon. He too is represented as a snake.

Why Zeus was the protector of the house is clear if we consider the epithet "father," which is very often given to him by the Greeks, the Indians, the Illyrians,[11] and the Romans, in whose language the epithet coalesced with the noun to form the name "Jupiter." The occurrence of this epithet among these four peoples of Indo-European stock proves that it is an ancient heritage from the time before they had separated. It is generally supposed to designate Zeus as father of gods and men, but this is clearly erroneous. It cannot be believed that in those ancient times, before the Indo-European peoples separated and began their great migrations, there was a nobility which traced its pedigree back to the gods as Homeric heroes did. Nor did Zeus create man or the world. He is neither creator nor father of men in the physical sense. Consequently,

---

[11] Hesychius s.v. Δειπάτυρος· ὁ θεὸς παρὰ Τυμφαίοις. The Tymphaeans were a tribe in Epirus.

the epithet must designate him as *pater familias*, the head of the family, which perfectly agrees with the patriarchal social conditions of the Indo-European peoples. And this is the reason why Zeus was the obvious protector of the house.

But the astonishing fact is that Zeus appears as a snake. This Zeus was, of course, called by modern scholars a chthonian deity, because the snake is always considered to represent the souls of the dead. Certainly it does so very often, but we may question whether this is always the case. It was once supposed that all family and domestic cults had sprung from the cult of the dead. This doctrine should be reduced to its proper proportions. It would surely be astonishing if the house cult had no other roots than the cult of the dead. Among many European peoples, as well as in other parts of the world, we find the snake as the guardian of the house. In my own country —Sweden—the house snake was extremely common, and only a few years ago there died a farmer of whom I know that he was wont to offer milk to the house snakes. The house snake is still generally venerated in the Balkan Peninsula and in modern Greece. When it appears it is greeted with reverent words, such as "welcome, lady of the house," "your obedient servant," "guardian," or "guardian spirit of our house." It is related that in ancient Egypt the houses were full of snakes, which were so tame that they came to partake of offerings when they were called. The Minoan snake-goddess was a house goddess.[12] She was a snake-goddess, not because, as Sir Arthur Evans asserts, she was the lady of the nether world and of the dead, but because she was a house goddess. The guardian spirit of the house had been anthropomorphized, and the house snake had become her attribute. Kipling, in "Letting in the Jungle," says of the doomed village: "Who could fight against the jungle, when the very village cobra had left his

---

[12] See my *Minoan-Mycenaean Religion*, pp. 279 ff.

hole in the platform under the peepul." The holy snake of Athena also went away when the Athenians evacuated their city at the coming of the Persians, as Herodotus reports. Athena was the house goddess of the Mycenaean king. She inherited the snake from the Minoan house goddess. The great goddess had statues, and the snake could be given to her as her attribute, but in the common house cult there were no statues or even statuettes. Hence, it seems that the house god Zeus himself appeared as a snake. But in reality the association is rather loose and came about because Zeus was the protector of the house and the snake was its guardian spirit in bodily form. Many snakes may live in a house, and therefore people sometimes called them the sons of Zeus, the *Dios kouroi*. In the cult of the house snake we have come upon another striking similarity between modern folklore and ancient Greek popular religion. We see how modern folklore is helpful to a correct understanding of Greek popular religion. The cult of the house snake also survives in modern Greece.

In the middle of the great living room of the Greek house, the megaron, was a fixed hearth. The fire of this hearth warmed the house on cold days, and over this fire meals were prepared. The fixed hearth was brought to Greece by the Greeks, for in Minoan houses there were only portable fire pots of the sort used for preparing meals in Hellenistic and even in modern times.[13] The sanctity of the hearth is common to the Greeks and the Romans, and it is very probable that the Greek name of the goddess of the hearth, Hestia, and her Roman name, Vesta, are both derived from the same word, although this has been contested.[14] The sanctity of the hearth

[13] In early Minoan times there seems sometimes to have been a fixed hearth; later only portable fire pots existed. See P. Demargne, "Culte funéraire et foyer domestique dans la Crète minoenne," *Bulletin de correspondance hellénique,* LVI (1932), 60 ff.

[14] By F. Solmsen, *Untersuchungen zur griechischen Laut- und Verslehre* (Strassburg, 1901), pp. 191, 213.

is bound up with the fixed hearth. Consequently, the Greeks are responsible for it, not the pre-Greek population, who did not have a fixed hearth. The hearth is the center of the house and the symbol of the family. When Herodotus counts the number of families in a town he counts the hearths.[15] The hearth was sacred. A suppliant took his place on the hearth, as did Odysseus, Telephus, and Themistocles, because he was protected by its sanctity. People swore by the hearth. The newborn babe was received into the family by being carried around the hearth, a ceremony which was called *amphidromia* and took place on the fifth day after birth.

The hearth was the center of the house cult and of the piety of daily life. We should remember that while our piety is expressed chiefly in words, by prayers, the piety of the ancients was expressed chiefly by acts. In our schools the day begins with a morning prayer, but in the Greek gymnasia there was a hero shrine at which cult rites were performed. This fact is particularly evident in daily life. Whereas we say a prayer before and after the meal, the Greeks before the meal offered a few bits of food on the hearth and after it poured out a few drops of unmixed wine on the floor. The libation was said to be made to Agathos Daimon, the Good Daemon, the guardian of the house, who appears in snake form. It is not stated to whom the food offering was made, but if someone is to be mentioned it must be Hestia, the goddess of the hearth.

Thus, the hearth was sacred, and the daily meal was sacred. The sanctity of the meal found expression in the rites which accompanied it. It is a widespread custom to regard the meal as sacred. Among many peoples a stranger who has been permitted to take part in a meal is thereby received under the protection of the tribe and becomes inviolable. The meal unites with sacred bonds all who partake of it. One may recall the old Russian custom of offering a distinguished visitor bread and

---

[15] Herodotus, I, 177.

salt before the gates of the city. The same feeling was alive in Greece. "Thou hast forsaken thy great oath, the table, and the salt," the poet Archilochus says reproachfully to someone;[16] and the orator Aeschines asked emphatically of his colleagues by whom he thought he had been deceived: "Where is the salt? where the table? where the drink-offering?"[17]

This sanctity of the meal, which knits the partakers together in a sacred community, will help us to understand the best known and most prominent of all the rites of Greek religion, animal sacrifice. Its meaning and origin have been vigorously discussed. A great scholar, W. Robertson Smith, advanced the hypothesis of a totemistic origin.[18] The animal sacrificed was the god himself, Smith thought, and by eating his flesh the worshippers were united with the god and imbued with his power. This hypothesis has been somewhat modified by Jane Harrison[19] and others, but it is untenable. Not the slightest trace of totemism appears among the Greeks or other Indo-European peoples. The sacredness of the meal suffices to explain the peculiarities of animal sacrifice. The sacrifice is a meal common to the god and his worshippers, linking them together in a close unity. The god is invited by prayer to come to the meal. He receives his portion, and the men, who are the greater number, feast on their portions. This is the reason why only a small portion of the flesh is offered on the altar of the god, a custom which had already struck Hesiod as so peculiar that he invented a mythical explanation of it.[20] The sacrifice is sacred. This is the reason why it is often forbidden to carry parts of it outside the holy precinct. Even the refuse, the bones,

---

[16] Frag. 96, in Bergk, *Poetae lyrici Graeci.*
[17] Demosthenes, XIX, 189.
[18] *Lectures on the Religion of the Semites,* 3d ed. (London, 1927).
[19] *Prolegomena,* pp. 84 ff.
[20] *Theogony,* vss. 535 ff. See Ada Thomsen, "Der Trug des Prometheus," *Archiv für Religionswissenschaft,* XII (1909), 460 ff.

and the ashes are sacred and are left in the sanctuary. Such a sacrifice was performed not only at festivals but occasionally in daily life. Whenever an animal was slaughtered, it was considered as a sacrifice and was accompanied by the usual rites. The word *philothytes* (fond of sacrifices) signifies simply "hospitable."

The sanctity of the hearth was not conferred by any god but was immanent. Hestia was never wholly anthropomorphized. She was given a place in mythology, but her statues are artistic inventions, not cult statues. Nevertheless, her importance was great. A Greek proverb says: "Begin with Hestia," that is to say, "Begin at the right end." If an animal was slaughtered and a sacrifice was performed in the house, the first pieces of the sacrificial meal were offered to her, just as at all meals a few pieces were laid on the hearth. This is the reason why it seems to have been customary to offer the first pieces of all sacrifices, even public ones, to Hestia. The position of Hestia is also reflected in semiphilosophical speculations, in which it is said that Hestia is enthroned in the middle of the universe, just as the hearth is the center of the house.

A few words must be added concerning the role of the hearth in public cult, for this role is the best argument for the belief that the family was the model and basis of Greek state organization. Just as each family had its hearth, so the state had its hearth in the council house, where the officials and a few especially honored citizens took their daily meals. When a colony was founded, the emigrants carried fire from this hearth to kindle the fire on the hearth of the new city.

The cult of the hearth comes down from hoary antiquity, from Indo-European times. It induces me to add a remark of general bearing in regard to the difference between our religion and that of the Greeks, especially their popular religion. This difference is less appreciated than it ought to be, because our attitude is not the same as that of the Greeks. The sanctity of the hearth was great, and we rightly speak of a cult of the hearth because certain sacred acts were performed there. But there were no prayers, no images, and no gods, for Hestia herself was not a full-fledged personality but only a pale personification. The cult consisted in acts. The place was sacred in itself according to the ideas of the ancients. For us it is not so. Nowadays a place is made sacred by erecting a house of God on it. Sanctity is conferred upon the building by its consecration as a church. In antiquity sanctity was inherent in the place. The place was not made holy by building a house for a god on it, but a house for a god was built on a certain place because the place was holy. Finally, although the hearth was sacred, the same hearth was used for nonreligious purposes—for roasting meat and cooking food, for boiling water and heating the room. Here we come upon another difference between ancient and modern religious ideas, which is perhaps greater than any other. We make a clear distinction between the sacred and the profane, we object to using holy things for ordinary purposes. Religion is our Sunday suit. The ancients also made a distinction between the sacred and the profane. Sacred things could not be treated as profane things. But the sacred and the profane were intermingled in daily life in a manner of which there are almost incredible examples. Religion was much more a part of daily life among the ancients than among us. It consisted in acts more than in words. Obviously, there was a danger that these acts might become a mere routine, and in general they probably did. They were deprived of real religious feeling even more than our grace is when it is recited by custom and without thinking.

The sanctity of the hearth was so great that everyone who sat on it was sacred and could not be violated. One would probably say that he was under the protection of the gods. This was, in fact, considered to be so, but the statement is not quite correct. The hearth was sacred in itself, and its sacredness was conferred upon anybody touching it. There was no question of any personal god as mediator. But, on the other hand, everyone who sought protection at the hearth was under the protection of the gods and, it should be added, of a quite special god, Zeus. This takes us back to early times, in which law and justice and the state were only slightly developed. Divine protection to foreigners and suppliants was much more important then than in historical times, when life was regulated by state institutions and laws and was relatively secure. It should be added that respect for certain religious rules in regard to foreigners and suppliants is found among most primitive peoples, and such rules must have existed in very ancient Indo-European times.

Under primitive conditions a foreigner is excluded from the protection of law and custom enjoyed by members of the tribe. The word "guest" and the Latin word *hostis* (foe) are the same word. A suppliant is a man who by trespassing against law and custom has put himself outside their protection. Such a man might be purified and pardoned. As for foreigners, there might be reasons for entering into friendly relations with them. They might, for example, be merchants, for trade, however restricted, always existed, even in early times and under the most primitive conditions. From ancient times there was a god who conferred his protection upon foreigners and suppliants, namely, Zeus. He, and almost he alone, has epithets referring to this function (*xenios, hikesios*), and they were very commonly used in the historical age. Zeus was the protector of suppliants and foreigners because he, being "the father," the divine *pater familias*, upheld the unwritten laws and customs on which the power of the head of the family depended. Such laws and customs were necessary, for otherwise a person who had trespassed would not have been able to make atonement, nor would commerce or other relations with people outside the tribe have been possible. So Zeus was the protector of the unwritten laws, of the moral order, and of customs invested with religious sanctity in primitive Greek society. But as political life gradually developed and life became more secure, this function of Zeus receded into the background in actual practice. Generally speaking, people did not need to turn to Zeus for protection. Theoretically, Zeus always remained the heavenly ruler and the protector of justice and morality, but hardly more than theoretically.

From of old, Zeus had been the protector of the house, the family, and its rights. But as the power of the state increased and internal peace was secured, life became safer and consequently the importance of Zeus in private life diminished. Zeus Ktesios and Zeus Herkeios remained, but not much was said of them. The old rites were performed in a routine fashion, more or less without thought. The importance of Zeus and his cult was noticeably less in the classical age than in Homer. He was still officially the highest god, the protector of the state and of the law. But in daily life people cared more for other gods who were nearer to them.

If in historical times people were relatively safe from the assaults of enemies and from robbery, they feared dangers of other kinds which threatened them and their houses. Belief in magic and witchcraft is primeval and was not lacking even in the classical age. The house also had to be protected against secret perils from these sources, and for this purpose people resorted to gods who were able to avert evils of all kinds. One of these was the great hero Heracles, who had vanquished so many monsters, ghosts (Antaeus was a ghost), and even Death. Above the entrance to the house was placed the inscription: "Here the gloriously triumphant Heracles dwells; here let no evil enter."

Another great averter of evil was Apollo, the god of sanctity and purifications. A connection with the cult of stones was peculiar to this god, and holy stones were common in Greece. Xenophon speaks of certain men who did not venerate temples or altars and of others who venerated stones, pieces of wood, and animals.[21] Theophrastus mentions superstitious people who poured oil on stones standing at the crossroads, fell on their knees before them, and greeted them with a kiss of the hand.[22] The omphalos of Apollo at Delphi is especially famous. In origin it was neither a tomb nor the center of the world, but simply one holy stone among many which was made famous by the fame of the god. Holy stones stood before the doors of houses. Perhaps they did in prehistoric times also. Square-cut stones have been found before the gates of the Homeric Troy by Dörpfeld, as well as by recent American excavators.[23] Since they could have served no practical purpose, it is supposed that their purpose was religious. We may perhaps venture to go further. Hrozný has published the inscriptions of four Hittite altars and read their pictographs.[24] Among other gods there is mentioned one whose name is read *Apulunas*. He is a god of the gates. If this be so, then the oriental origin of Apollo, which has often been asserted but which has also been vehemently contested, is proved beyond doubt. This oriental Apollo was the protector of the gates; so was the Apollo of classical Greece.

Before every Greek house a high conical stone was erected

[21] *Memorabilia*, I, 1, 14.

[22] *Characteres*, 16.

[23] W. Dörpfeld, *Troja und Ilion* (Athens, 1902), p. 134 and Figs. 44, 45; C. W. Blegen in *Amer. Journ. of Archaeology*, XXXVIII (1934), 241, Fig. 18, and XLI (1937), 593, Fig. 36.

[24] B. Hrozný, "Les Quatre Autels 'hittites' hiéroglyphiques d'Emri Ghazi et d'Eski Kisla," *Archiv orientalin*, VIII (1936), 171 ff.

(Fig. 30). It was called Apollo Agyieus (Apollo of the street) because it stood in the street before the door of the house. Oil was poured on it, and it was decorated with fillets. Hence, it was sometimes called an altar, and sometimes an altar was erected at its side. We do not know whether the holy stone is older than Apollo himself. At all events, the stone protected the house against evil, and in the classical age it was sacred to Apollo, the great averter of evil.

Before the house an image of the triple Hecate was very often erected (Fig. 33). Aristophanes tells us that when a woman left her house she made a prayer to Hecate.[25] We shall have more to say of this goddess later. The Greeks always regarded her as the special goddess of magic and witchcraft. A power that can produce ghosts and magical evils can also avert them, and this is the reason why images of Hecate were set up at crossroads and before houses.

In this chapter I have dealt with the religion of the house and the family. I may perhaps pertinently conclude it by a few words about the social aspect of ancient Greek religion. In contrast to oriental peoples and to some others, the Greeks had no professional priests and no temples with their own property and administration. The head of the family was the priest of his house and the king was the high priest of the state as long as kingship existed and longer; for when the political power was taken from the king, he was usually allowed to keep his religious duties. Even if professionals, such as seers and sacrificial priests, were called in, they were only advisers. From the beginning, religion and society, or the state, were not two separate entities among the Greeks but two closely related aspects of the same entity.

If we consider these facts, an unexpected question emerges. The house cult was only a small part of Greek religion. Who

[25] *Lysistrata,* vs. 64.

looked after all the other cults of the gods in the old days? Of course many of the cults, including some which might have been inherited from the Mycenaean age, were under the care of the king. Furthermore, we must not attribute to earlier times great temples and statues like those of the classical age. The cult places were groves, springs, caves, and the like, with a simple altar of unworked stones or sods. We hear of this state of things in Homer, who relates that sacrifices were performed at a spring beneath a plane tree and that votive gifts were suspended from the branches of the trees in the grove. If such a cult place became popular and was visited by many people and if the god received many gifts, a small building was erected to house him and his paraphernalia. This is what we mean when we speak of a temple of those times. A building of this sort might be erected by the people in common. But in several cases we know that the cult was under the care of a certain family, which was, of course, the family owning the ground where the cult place was.

A great many cults were the property of a certain family. We know that this was true in Attica,[26] about which our information is much better than about other states of Greece, and we may suppose that the same was true everywhere. To adduce some examples, the Eleusinian Mysteries belonged to the Eumolpidae; the Mysteries at Phlya belonged to the Lycomidae; the priestess of Athena Polias and the priest of Poseidon in the Erechtheum were taken from the Eteobutadae, whence it is inferred that this family was the old royal house of Athens; and the Bouzygae performed the sacred plowing at the foot of the Acropolis. Herodotus says that he does not know the origin of Isagoras, the rival of Cleisthenes, but that

[26] The examples are collected by J. Toepffer, *Attische Genealogie* (Berlin, 1889).

his family sacrificed to Zeus Karios.[27] A certain cult was characteristic of a certain family.

Such a state of things is characteristic of the rule of the nobility, to whom the political power belonged at the commencement of the archaic age. The lower classes, the people without ancestors, turned to modest rural sanctuaries or even to the cults maintained by the nobility, on whom they were dependent. They apparently formed a kind of cult association, of which the members were called *orgeones* (worshippers). In regard to the cult, Solon seems to have put these associations on an equal footing with the noble families.[28] The noble families were divided into phratries, or brotherhoods, whose members were called *phrateres* (brothers). The political reforms of Solon and Cleisthenes democratically extended this organization to the people without ancestors. Every Athenian citizen belonged to a brotherhood. This political reorganization must have involved a reorganization of the family cult.

I have already said that the newly elected Athenian archons were asked if they possessed a Zeus Herkeios, an Apollo Patroos, and family tombs and where these were situated. Zeus Herkeios was, as we have seen, the protector of the courtyard. Apollo Patroos was the *agyieus*, the stone pillar erected before the door of the house. The purpose of these questions was to ascertain that the man was a citizen. In an age when written records were unknown, citizenship was proved by the ownership of a house and ground. Such proof could be given only by men who owned landed property. But the people without ancestors had no landed property. The democratic reform did not alter the form of the examination, but it altered the form of the cult so that it embraced all the people. The old house gods were taken over by the phratries. The phratries maintained

---

[27] Herodotus, V, 66.
[28] See my *Gesch. der griech. Rel.,* I, 672.

a cult of the gods of the phratries. These gods were called *patrooi* (inherited from the ancestors) or *phratrioi* (gods of the brotherhood). The Athenians venerated Zeus Herkeios, whom others called Patroos or Phratrios, and Apollo Patroos, who was supposed to be the mythical ancestor of the Athenian people. To these was added the city goddess Athena with the epithet of Phratia.

It may perhaps be objected that the matters just mentioned do not belong to popular religion as we understand it. But in ancient Greece they did, for the cult of the phratry gods was the cult of all the people, since it was the cult of the small subdivisions of the Attic state. The origin of these gods is to be found in the family and house cult. This cult is little known. In the classical age it consisted mainly of the daily routine, and its importance vanished when politics and the great cults became predominant. The aim of this chapter has been to reveal its fundamental significance for a correct understanding of the religion and the life of the Greek people.

THE CITIES; THE
PANEGYREIS

IN A PREVIOUS CHAPTER I STRONGLY EMPHASIZED THE
fact that in early times Greece was a country of tillers of the
soil and of herdsmen, who subsisted on the products of their
own labor. To these, of course, we must add the owners of
the great landed estates, the nobility. But I have not forgotten
that Greece was also a country of city-states. In some of the
towns industrial and commercial activities were started, and
these towns played the leading role in the development of
Greek culture and even in religion. In the eighth and seventh
centuries B.C. Greece was apparently overpopulated. The
products of its soil were not sufficient for the increasing number
of its inhabitants. We know from Hesiod how straitened were
the circumstances of the small farmers. The stress was re-
lieved not only by emigration and the founding of colonies
around the Mediterranean, but also by the rise of industry
and commerce in certain towns. At that time the laborers in
the many workshops were not slaves, as they were in the
classical age. The poor country population crowded into the
towns, where they could find work and earn a livelihood which,
although poor, was more certain than that provided by the
seasonal labor of agriculture. This is the background of the
social and political changes of the early historical age in
Greece. The power of the nobility broke down. In the towns
which were ahead in the development of industry and com-

merce tyrants arose. The rule of the tyrants was founded on the broad mass of the city population, and the tyrants strove to promote the interests of the masses. But this was only an interlude. The tyrants were expelled before the early age reached its end, and democracy, or at least a mitigated aristocracy, was established.[1]

After this time the cities were the leaders in Greek culture, although many parts of Greece remained rural and backward. We have heard how the cities took over parts of the old rural religion in their festivals and modified them accordingly. The great gods, who protected the state and the citizens, had their home in the city, and their greatness was enhanced by art and literature. We should not forget these gods, but we should also like to know what the man in the street thought and what he believed in. There was a popular religion of the townspeople also, though little is said of it.

The great gods of the Greeks came down from various peoples and ages. Some of them were derived from the pre-Greek population, others were Greek, and still others were immigrants. Most of them were very complex. Many of them were venerated by the rural population. We have met several of them already. But the cults of the countryside were not responsible for their greatness. For this they were indebted to the cults of the cities and to art and literature. According to Herodotus,[2] Homer and Hesiod created the Greek gods, and this statement is true to a certain degree. Homer impressed his representations of the gods indelibly on the Greek mind. I may add that the great temples of the gods adorned with works of art were, of course, erected in the cities, except for a few erected in places which attracted a

---

[1] See my Dill lecture, *The Age of the Early Greek Tyrants* (Belfast, 1936).
[2] Herodotus, II, 53.

stream of visitors for special reasons—Olympia, Delphi, Delos, and at a later time Epidaurus. I shall return to these later. The sanctuaries described by Homer were simple rustic sanctuaries—an altar in a grove, on the trees of which votive offerings were suspended. Great temples were erected at the earliest in the seventh century B.C. That there was a certain connection between this building activity and the rule of the tyrants was already remarked by Aristotle, who says that the tyrants erected great buildings in order to give occupation to the people. Their wish to make a show of their power and glory was certainly another reason. The great temple at Corinth, of which seven heavy columns are still standing, belongs to the age of the tyrants.[3] At Athens, Pisistratus rebuilt the temple of Athena on a magnificent scale and began building a colossal temple of Zeus Olympios.

Very little is known concerning the policies of the tyrants in religious matters, but we can be sure that they followed the course along which democracy proceeded further, that of humoring the people by instituting elaborate festivals and games. This is known to be true of Athens, where Pisistratus introduced the Great Dionysia and made considerable additions to the magnificent celebration of the Panathenaea.

After the great victory over the Persians, Athens took the lead in commerce and culture. Its people were, of course, proud of its great achievements and of the empire which it had acquired. Patriotic and even chauvinistic feelings sprang up, and in this age they could find expression only in religion. The state and the gods were a unity. The gods had given victory, power, and glory to the Athenian state. The Athenians gloried in being the most pious of all peoples and in celebrating

---

[3] S. Weinberg in *Hesperia*, VIII (1939), 191 ff., seems on archaeological grounds to have proved that this temple was built about 540 B.C. and that it was preceded by an earlier temple.

the most numerous and magnificent festivals in honor of the gods. They were able to do this because they could afford the costs. Great sacrifices, in which hundreds of animals were sometimes slaughtered, accompanied the cult observances. Portions of the sacrifices were distributed among the people, who were even permitted to take them home. The people feasted at the expense of the gods, and they soon learned the advantages of this kind of piety. The great temples erected in this age, of which the most famous is the Parthenon, enhanced not only the glory of the gods but also the glory of the capital of the empire.

In the long run this kind of religion was no boon to the great gods. Religion was to a certain degree secularized. When Aristophanes mentions the festivals, he speaks only of the feasting and the markets connected with them, and in one passage he refers to certain ceremonies of the Dipolia as to something antediluvian.[4] The great gods became greater and more glorious, but religious feeling gave way to feelings of patriotism and to display in festivals and sacrifices. The state gods, the great gods, thus became more remote from human beings. We shall soon see examples of this in the case of the city goddess Athena.

The population of the large industrial and commercial towns consisted to a great extent of laborers, or, to speak more exactly, of artisans, for the ancient factories were mere workshops and the methods of production were those of handicraft. The crafts also needed divine protection. We know a little about this, especially in regard to one craft which was of extreme importance in this age, that of the potter. It gave its name to a large district in the city of Athens, the Kerameikos. In the seventh century it was of equal importance at Corinth. From the beginning the potters addressed them-

---

[4] *Nubes*, vs. 984.

selves to the great gods of the town. In a sanctuary of Poseidon at Corinth was found a great mass of painted clay tablets, some of which represent scenes connected with the potters' art—the making and firing of vessels, their exportation, and so forth.[5] The tablets are votive offerings dedicated to Poseidon by potters.

The potters feared lesser gods and daemons who might destroy their work. Among the relics of popular poetry preserved in the biography of Homer ascribed to Herodotus there is a potters' song. It begins with a prayer that Athena may hold her hand over the potters' oven, and that the vessels may be well fired, receive a beautiful black color, and yield a good profit when they are sold. But if the potters do not reward the poet, he conjures up daemons to destroy the vessels in the oven: Smaragos, who makes them crack; Syntrips, who smashes them; Asbestos, the inextinguishable one; Sabaktes, who shatters them; and Omodamos. The significance of the last is not clear, though the first part of the compound refers to crude clay. Finally the poet threatens to bring in the witch Circe and the ferocious centaurs. He uses the common mythology, of course; but it is interesting to note not only that Athena is the potters' protectress, but also, and especially, that the potters believed in a lot of mischievous goblins which were apt to destroy their work. Perhaps some such goblin is depicted on one of the tablets from the sanctuary of Poseidon.

In Athens, Athena was the protectress of the artisans. This was quite natural, for she was already so in Homer. She protected the weaving of the women and the art of the goldsmiths and the coppersmiths. An Attic vase shows her in a potter's workshop (Fig. 34). For the popularity of Athena among the artisans at this time some verses of Sophocles are

[5] Published in *Antike Denkmäler*, II (1908), Pls. 23, 24.

characteristic: "Come out in the street you, all the people of the handicraftsmen, who venerate the daughter of Zeus, Ergane, with sacrificial baskets and beside the heavy anvil, beaten with hammers."[6] Evidently Sophocles hints at some popular festival of Athena celebrated by the artisans in the streets of the town. There was such a festival, the Chalkeia. The word signifies the festival of the coppersmiths. It belonged to Athena, but at a later date another god of the Athenian artisans, Hephaistos, was associated with Athena.[7] These two even had a common temple. In Homer, Hephaistos is the divine goldsmith. He probably came from the island of Lemnos or, perhaps, from Asia Minor. In origin he was a daemon of fire coming up from the earth. Gas which takes fire and burns is considered by many peoples to be divine. Later a volcano was considered to be his smithy. He had almost no cults in Greece except in Athens. No doubt the Athenian artisans took up his cult and placed him at the side of Athena. He seemed, perhaps, to be nearer to them than the great city goddess. But in the early age it was she who was the protectress of the Athenian craftsmen.

Many thousand shards of vases have been found in the debris left on the Acropolis after its devastation by the Persians; some of these vases were certainly dedicated by their makers. In the same debris a great many inscriptions have been found on bases on which votive gifts had been placed. Among the people who set them up were craftsmen. From the point of view taken here their diminishing number in later times is very significant. The second and third volumes of the Attic inscriptions, which commence with the year 403 B.C., contain only thirty-three dedications to Athena, and of these

[6] Frag. 760, in Nauck, *Tragicorum Graecorum fragmenta.*
[7] L. Malten, "Hephaistos," *Jahrbuch des Deutschen archäol. Instituts,* XXVII (1912), 232 ff.

twenty-two belong to the fourth century B.C., one to the Hellenistic age, and ten to the Roman age.[8] The few inscriptions from the time after 403 B.C. reflect the decline of Athenian industry and Athenian importance, but the small number from the fourth century B.C. is also significant. It cannot be explained except on the ground that Athena had become too exalted to be a goddess of the common people.

Man needs gods who are near to him. In the countryside there were minor gods to whom the simple peasants prayed and made offerings. There were minor gods in the town also, and they were certainly venerated. But these minor gods were too insignificant; they were not able to satisfy the human need for divine help and protection. When a gap exists it is usually filled, and as the Greek gods did not meet the needs of the Greek people, other gods were brought in from other peoples with whom the Greeks had intercourse. First came Hecate from the southwestern corner of Asia Minor, as early as the early archaic age. Propaganda was resorted to on behalf of her cult, as is apparent in the *Homeric Hymn to Demeter* and in a long passage inserted into Hesiod's *Theogony*, in which she is praised as omnipotent.[9] That Hecate originated in Caria is proved by the fact that proper names compounded with her name are very frequent in this district and rare or absent elsewhere.[10] We do not know what kind of goddess Hecate was in Caria. In Greece the attempt to make a great goddess of her did not succeed. She was always the goddess of witchcraft and sorcery who walked at the crossroads on moonless nights, accompanied by evil ghosts and barking dogs. Offerings were thrown out to her at the crossroads, and her image was triple because she had to look

[8] Noted by A. Körte in *Gnomon*, XI (1935), 639.
[9] *Theogony*, vss. 411-52.
[10] E. Sittig, *De Graecorum nominibus theophoris* (Dissertation, Halle, 1911), pp. 61 ff.

in three directions. She was often called Enodia (she of the roads). Some scholars think that Enodia was a native Greek goddess of witchcraft,[11] but their arguments are not very convincing. At all events Hecate was accepted by the Greeks because there was a place for a goddess of witchcraft and ghosts. Her popularity is accounted for by this fact, and it proves that base superstition was only too common among the Greeks.

The Greeks also knew about other gross and uncanny specters: Mormo, with whom imprudent nurses were wont to frighten small children; Gello; Karko; Sybaris; Empousa, who according to Aristophanes was able to change herself into a beast, a dog, a snake, or a fair woman; Onoskelis, who had an ass's leg. These monsters attacked men, sucked their blood, and ate their entrails. Educated people did not trouble about them, but they found a refuge in nursery tales and were cherished by the people. It is characteristic that they became still more popular in the Roman age, during which superstition continually increased. A generic name for such beings was lamia, and whereas the great gods are forgotten, the lamia still lives on among the Greek people. The lamia is mentioned in the Middle Ages, and nowadays it is customary to frighten children with the name. If a child dies suddenly, it is said that the lamia strangled it. An ugly or insatiable woman is called a lamia.[12] Such ghosts seem to be immortal. The gods were not so.

We return to the foreign gods who migrated into Greece. The Great Mother of Asia Minor came to Athens before the Persian Wars, and a temple, the Metroon, was built for her[13]

[11] U. von Wilamowitz-Moellendorff, *Der Glaube der Hellenen* (Berlin, 1931-32), I, 169 ff.

[12] Lawson, *Modern Greek Folklore and Ancient Greek Religion,* pp. 173 ff.

[13] See my forthcoming *Gesch. der griech. Rel.,* I, 687 ff.

(Fig. 35). Pindar celebrates her and mentions her orgiastic cult with its cymbals, castanets, and torches.[14] He also celebrates Ammon, the god from the Great Oasis who had ram's horns, knowledge of whom was probably transmitted by the Cyrenaeans, for from Cyrene there was a road to the Great Oasis.[15] His oracle was frequented by the Greeks when their belief in their own oracles began to wane, and the Athenians brought him a sacrifice on behalf of the state in the fourth century B.C. These cults seem, however, not to have been very important for popular belief. The Great Mother was thoroughly assimilated to the Greek Mother, Demeter, and her cult lost its orgiastic character. In this case there was a return to native customs. Ammon seems hardly to have been popular in the strict sense of the word.

Other foreign gods were popular. The Cabiri[16] are mentioned in the fifth century B.C. Aristophanes, in his comedy *The Peace*, makes Trygaios turn to the spectators and ask the help of those who had been initiated into the mysteries of the Cabiri on the island of Samothrace, for he sees a great storm approaching. There must have been such men in the audience and the mysteries of the Cabiri must have been well known. The Cabiri were venerated by the Greeks as protectors of seafarers. Although they were a seafaring people, the Greeks were apparently not content with their own sea-gods.

The Thracian goddess Bendis was introduced by Thracians living at Peiraeus (Fig. 36). She was so respected that the state approved a great festival for her, which is described

[14] For Magna Mater see Pindar, *Pythia,* III, vss. 77 ff., and frags. 79, 80, 95, in Bergk, *Poetae lyrici Graeci.*

[15] For Ammon see Pausanias, IX, 16, 1.

[16] See O. Kern, "Kabeiros und Kabeiroi," in A. Pauly, *Real-encyclopädie der classischen Altertumswissenschaft,* new ed. by G. Wissowa (Stuttgart, 1894-).

by Plato,[17] and paid large sums for sacrifices to her. There is, however, nothing to indicate that she had any real religious importance. Another Thracian goddess, Kotyto, was perhaps a little more popular at Corinth and in Sicily.[18] One of the rites in her cult was baptism, and her cult seems to have had an orgiastic character. The Phrygian god Sabazios, who was another form of Dionysus, is better known because of the graphic description of his cult in Demosthenes' speech against Aeschines. He is mentioned by Aristophanes also. Demosthenes says that Aeschines read the holy books when his mother performed the initiations, wore a fawnskin at night, mixed the wine, purified those who were to be initiated, wiped them with clay and bran, and made them rise and cry out, "I escaped the evil, I found the better." By day he led the crowds through the streets, crowned with fennel and poplar twigs, carried snakes in his hands, danced, and cried out: *euoi, saboi*. Scenes like this were to be seen in the streets of Athens at that time. Apparently, not a few people felt the appeal of such orgiastic cults.

Very characteristic of the age is the sudden rise of the cult of Asclepius at the end of the fifth century B.C. (Fig. 38). He was a healing hero, mentioned by Homer only as the father of the surgeons Machaon and Podaleirios. Apollo was the great god of healing for the Greeks, but in many places various heroes served as gods of healing, like the saints in Mohammedan countries today. Asclepius supplanted them all. His most famous sanctuary was at Epidaurus, but he had many derivative cults (Fig. 37). There was one on the island of Aegina, one at Sicyon, one at Delphi, one at Pergamum, and no less than three in Attica—one at Peiraeus, one near

[17] *Republic*, p. 327; and *Inscriptiones Graecae*, Editio minor, Vols. II-III, Pt. 2, No. 1436, A, a, l. 86, and b, l. 117.
[18] S. Srebrny, "Kult der thrakischen Göttin Kotyto in Korinth und Sicilien," *Mélanges Franz Cumont* (Brussels, 1936), pp. 423 ff.

Eleusis, and one on the southern slope of the Acropolis. He came to Athens in 420 B.C., being introduced by Telemachos of Acharnae and received by the poet Sophocles, who because of this was made a hero under the name of Dexion, the Receiver. All these derivative cults, founded within a brief space of time, did not interfere with the growth of his chief cult at Epidaurus. In the secluded valley in which the sanctuary was situated, buildings of an astonishingly large number and size were erected at the beginning of the fourth century B.C.—a temple adorned with sculptures by one of the best artists of the age, Timotheus, a very beautiful theatre, and the famous tholos. The costs, which were quite considerable, must have been defrayed by the income from the people who flocked to Epidaurus in order to be healed of their diseases.

The masses were perhaps materialistic in this age. The Sophists had begun to criticize belief in the gods and to prove its irrationality by arguments. Aristophanes and other comic poets mocked the gods in an incredible manner. The general public laughed at their jests and were somewhat impressed by the criticism of the Sophists, but the old belief lurked in the background. The Athenian people believed that the gods had given them victory and had created their empire. They knew the advantages of this, and they experienced them in the great mass sacrifices. Generally they treated the unbelievers and mockers leniently, but on certain occasions a real religious hysteria broke out. The most outstanding examples are the trials for the profanation of the Eleusinian Mysteries and for the smashing of the herms shortly before the Athenian fleet sailed for Sicily. Certainly these trials had a political background, and so had the other trials for denial of the gods. We shall come back to them later. The good Athenian citizens believed that they believed in the gods, but their belief was fading away.

But man needs divine help and comfort.[19] The great gods had become too exalted to give help in the concerns of daily life. Even if men were materialistic they still needed aid and solace at least in sickness. In our own day we have seen people stream to certain places and churches to which they are attracted by miraculous healings. In modern Greece they go to the famous Panagia Euangelistria on the island of Tenos. When human skill is of no avail, men put their trust in the divine, in miracles. At this time, when the old bonds imposed by tradition and the state were beginning to be loosened and broken, men were not content with the gods of the state and the family, with whom they were linked from birth. They sought new gods for themselves. If the gods of the ancestors could not help them, they turned to other gods. These circumstances explain the sudden popularity of Asclepius, the great healer and comforter in sickness and distress. They also explain why foreign gods began to migrate into Greece.

We have seen that certain of these foreign gods represented mystic and orgiastic cults. The Greek civic cult was sober and well regulated. There was not much in it that was orgiastic and mystic, with the exception of the Eleusinian Mysteries. But religion has its emotional side, and if this is repressed it finally breaks out. This is the reason why the cults mentioned took hold on some people, though in general they were despised. On the whole, women are more emotional than men, a fact which is very apparent in Greek religion. The Dionysiac orgies were suppressed in the historical age and were celebrated chiefly in art and literature, but there are traces enough to show that the Dionysiac frenzy had once spread like fire in dry grass and had especially affected the women.

[19] See my paper, "Reflexe von dem Durchbruch des Individualismus in der griechischen Religion um die Wende des 5. und 4. Jhts. v. Chr.," *Mélanges Franz Cumont*, pp. 365 ff.

Greek society was an extremely male society, especially in Athens and the Ionian cities. Women were confined to their houses and seldom went outdoors. But religion did not exclude them. There were priestesses in many cults, and women regularly took part in the festivals and sacrifices. Some festivals were reserved for them. Virgins carried the sacred implements and provisions at the sacrifices. These *kanephoroi*, as they were called, appeared in all processions. Women even had to be allowed to take part in certain nocturnal festivals. The violating of a virgin on such an occasion is a common motif in the New Comedy. Aristophanes informs us that the women were proud of the sacred ceremonies in which they had taken part.[20]

Nevertheless, women had only a subordinate position. Men had fashioned the religion according to their own ideas and had left too little room for emotionalism. The women had a longing for an emotional religion, and Aristophanes tells us that they found means of satisfying it. He says that when the women gathered in the sanctuaries of Bacchos, Pan, Genetyllis, or Kolias (Genetyllis and Kolias were special goddesses of women) it was hardly possible to get through because of the cymbals, and he gives us to understand that the women were devoted to the cults of Sabazios and Adonis.[21] Sabazios has already been mentioned. Adonis, according to the myth, was the beloved of Aphrodite and was killed in his youth while hunting. His cult came from the Orient and was highly emotional. One of the customs associated with the cult was the growing of plants in pots, where they sprouted quickly and soon withered (Fig. 39). They were symbolic of the vegetation cycle, which Adonis represented. The women bewailed him, tore their clothes,

[20] *Lysistrata,* vss. 641 ff.
[21] *Ibid.,* vss. 388 ff.

and beat their breasts. According to Plutarch, they did this when the Athenian fleet was about to sail for Sicily.[22]

It may be added that Hecate, the goddess of witchcraft, was one of the deities to whom the women were especially devoted. Aristophanes makes a woman pray to Hecate before the door when she leaves her house,[23] and he records a game performed by women in her honor.[24] The reason for her popularity with women is that in ancient Greece sorcery and witchcraft were the concern of women. It is a notable fact that we hear of witches but not of sorcerers.

Thus we see that the religion of the women had its special features in the classical age. It was much more emotional than the ordinary religion. Women had scarcely any influence on the religious development of this age, but one may guess that they contributed to the dissemination, which was then beginning, of mystic and orgiastic forms of religion.[25] In late antiquity such forms became increasingly popular. In the long run, therefore, the exclusion of women was disastrous to the old religion.

I wish now to discuss briefly a subject which students of Greek religion generally pass over lightly because it seems to have little to do with religion, although religion is its foundation. I mean the great festivals and meetings which the Greeks called *panegyreis* (gatherings of all).[26] They took place in some sacred precinct, they were dedicated to some god, and they were accompanied by sacrifices. In some of these gatherings games were the most important element. There were great festivals, huge sacrifices, and games in many cities—

[22] *Nicias,* 13, and *Alcibiades,* 18.

[23] *Lysistrata,* vs. 64.

[24] *Ibid.,* vs. 700.

[25] Cf. what is related of the mother of Aeschines by Demosthenes, XVIII, 259 ff., and of the priestess Ninos by Demosthenes, XVIII, 281 and scholion.

[26] Little attention has been paid to this subject. See my forthcoming *Gesch. der griech. Rel.,* I, 778 ff.

above all in the great and prosperous cities such as Athens—but properly speaking these were not panegyreis. It was characteristic of a panegyris that people flocked to it from more than one state. In fact people came from all neighboring towns and even from all Greece. The sanctuaries in which the panegyreis took place were thus in a certain measure common to all parts of the Greek race, although the sanctuaries were administered by the city in whose territory they were situated. This gave rise to conflicts. The control of the Olympic games was contested more than once. Pisa, to which Olympia belonged, was in early times conquered by the Eleans. Sometimes a league of neighboring states was formed in order to protect one of these sanctuaries. Such a league was called an amphictyony. Examples are the league of Calauria and, most famous of all, the league which took care of Delphi. The latter was originally formed in order to protect a small sanctuary of Demeter at Anthela near Thermopylae, but its protection was extended to the great sanctuary of Apollo at Delphi. Delphi was situated in the territory of Crisa. The Crisaeans were charged with harassing and extorting money from the pilgrims who went to Delphi. At any rate, there were conflicts, and in the early part of the sixth century B.C. a war broke out in which Crisa was destroyed. Delphi became free and was placed under the protection of the Amphictyons. Their part in the politics of a later age is well known and is of slight importance in this connection. I have recalled these facts in order to show how important these great assembly places were for what one might call the international life of the Greeks. The basis of their importance was religion.

The great games—the Olympia, the Pythia, the Isthmia, and the Nemea—were preëminently panegyreis in this sense. Most famous are the Olympic games. The interest in the games themselves was so great that one hardly thinks of the religious element. But we should bear in mind the great temples erected at Olympia, the great sacrifices offered, and the many cults attended to by numerous priests. All this is described at length by Pausanias. The celebration at Olympia was the largest panegyris of the Greeks. People from all towns and cities came together, and even the colonies took a large part in the assembly. The great games were of the highest importance for impressing upon the Greek mind a consciousness of the unity of the Greek nation. All men were admitted provided that they spoke Greek, although women were excluded. Anyone who had something on his mind that he wanted to lay before the nation found the best opportunity for doing so at the games. It was here that Gorgias, during the storms of the Peloponnesian War, exhorted the Greeks to concord. Here many other Sophists exhibited their art. Here also the rhapsodist Cleomenes is said to have recited to the public the *Katharmoi* of Empedocles. The importance of the Olympic games and similar assemblies for the development of national feeling and the cultivation of interrelationships and even for the cultural life of the Greeks can hardly be overestimated.

It must be added that a truce was proclaimed for a few months in order to make it possible for everyone to visit the great games. This was quite necessary, because the Greek cities were constantly warring against each other. A truce was likewise proclaimed on the occasion of the Eleusinian Mysteries. Among the Dorians the month of Karneios, in which the Karneia was celebrated, was a holy month, during which an armistice was to prevail. In the Hellenistic age several cities tried to institute panegyreis and to get them acknowledged by the other Greek states. Embassies were sent to such festivals from other states. Many inscriptions referring to such diplomatic exchanges have come down to us.

They were in some measure a substitute for large-scale politics, from which the Greek cities were excluded in that age.

At all panegyreis there were fairs, and in some cases the fair seems to have been the chief attraction. This was apparently so at the great panegyris on the island of Delos, at which all Ionians assembled. At the panegyris of the Aetolians at Thermos there was a great fair. Moreover, it seems that a market was held at all great festivals. Aristophanes speaks of them. Sometimes the word "panegyris" signifies simply "fair." In later times special regulations were made for these fairs. A motley sort of life took place at such assemblies. The great throng of people who collected together needed shelter and food, for a panegyris lasted several days. Tents and barracks were erected. *Skenein* (to set up a tent or barrack) is the common word for taking part in such an assembly. Hawkers and cooks set up their booths. Jugglers and acrobats gave exhibitions. At certain sanctuaries situated in remote and desert places buildings were erected to serve as lodginghouses and banquet halls.

Surely all this seems to have very little to do with religion. But the panegyreis had a religious foundation in the cult of the gods, and although they seem to be secular, they represent a side of Greek religion which should not be ignored. I may recall what I said earlier about the intimate relations between the cult of the gods and secular life in ancient Greece, relations which are of such a character that they sometimes astonish us. We are strongly under the influence of Protestant and Puritan ideas, which make a sharp division between matters pertaining to God and the affairs of our mundane life. They do not allow sacred and secular occupations to be intermingled. It is otherwise in southern Europe, and especially in Greece. Whoever has seen a modern Greek panegyris is strongly reminded of the ancient ones. The cult is new, being that of the Panagia or some saint, but the life is the same. Tents, bowers, and booths are erected, and the people feast and make merry. Of course religion has been secularized, but this form of religion, which seems to us hardly to be religion at all, has shown an extreme tenacity. It satisfies the need which men feel to get together, to enjoy themselves, to feast, and to make merry, and likewise the need of interrupting and lighting up the monotonous course of daily life. These are social needs which should not be overlooked, and Greek religion should not be blamed because it fulfilled them. In this respect it was more lasting than in any other.

In concluding this chapter I may remark that I have treated the changes which Greek popular religion underwent from a social point of view. The increase of the population in certain towns and the life of the towns remodeled the old rustic cults and made them insufficient for the new wants which arose through the change in social conditions. The development of the power and glory of the city exalted the great gods too far above the common people. Such people needed a religion which was nearer to them, gods who could help them in the affairs of daily life, and a cult in which the emotional element had its due share. The way was opened for new gods. On the other hand Greek religion did have a social aspect. The cult of the gods provided opportunities for assembling and feasting and for mutual intercourse between people from neighboring towns and even from all Greek countries. The panegyreis were an extremely important part of Greek social life, and the service which Greek religion rendered through them should not be undervalued.

LEGALISM AND SUPERSTITION; HELL

I HAVE SPOKEN OF THE RELIGION OF THE COUNTRYSIDE. Its cults certainly do not exhibit the gods in their highest aspects, nor do the rustic customs belong to the higher strata of religion. But they are near the bedrock of primitive ideas and they have survived the high gods, lasting on into our own day in Greece, as very similar forms of religion have in other European countries. I have spoken also of the religion of the townspeople. I have emphasized the fact that when a great number of people came together in a town and engaged in industry and commerce, their mode of life was profoundly changed as a result of their separation from nature and the cultivation of the soil and that as a consequence their religious needs and outlook also changed. There were other religious movements which were not a result of the difference between town and country, although they were connected with social conditions. This is especially true of the early age before the Persian Wars. I have said that this was, in part at least, an age of poverty and social distress. On the other hand it was an age of brisk and diversified activity, of sea voyages and colonization, of discoveries and of progress in all directions. The foundations of Greek science were laid at this time. Religion, too, was involved in these changes and developments. The new movements in Greek religion originated in this age, and they did not leave popular religion untouched.

In times of distress and need man is prone to seek relief and consolation in religion. The hardships of the age we are considering certainly intensified its religious movements and helped to spread certain ideas widely among the people. There are two main streams of contrasting ideas which appear in all religion, including that of the Greeks. Man may seek union with God in mystic and ecstatic forms of religion, or he may seek to make peace with God and win His favor by fulfilling His commandments to the last item. The latter is legalism. The mystic and ecstatic movement is well known and has often been expounded, as in the admirable and much read book by Erwin Rohde.[1] Its herald was Dionysus, whose popularity was based on the longing of humanity for mystic and ecstatic experiences. The violent diffusion of the Dionysiac orgies took place in so early an age that it has left traces only in myths and cults. When our historical information begins the Dionysiac frenzy had already been tamed by the joint activity of the state and the Delphic oracle. Mysticism was not dead, only repressed, and it took refuge in certain religious movements of an almost sectarian character, especially Orphism. Although these movements seem to have been widespread in the early age, they cannot be called popular in the strict sense of the word, and I must pass over them here.[2]

There were some very curious men, characteristic of this age, who were not unlike the medicine men of primitive peoples. They went around fasting and doing wonders, and their souls were able to leave their bodies, make journeys, and enter them again. At the same time they were purificatory priests connected with Apollo. They were mystics, of course,

---

[1] *Psyche; Seelencult und Unsterblichkeitsglaube der Griechen* (Freiburg i. B., 1894).

[2] See my paper, "Early Orphism and Kindred Religious Movements," *Harvard Theological Review*, XXVIII (1935), 181 ff.

but they were also associated with legalism, for purification from trespasses is a necessary complement of legalism and is imposed by it.

The legalistic tendency has been much less noticed than the mystical and ecstatic, but it is at least as important, and it finally carried the day in its higher, political forms. Here I propose to treat of its popular forms, which were in great part suppressed. We turn to the oldest work of Greek poetry next to Homer, Hesiod's *Works and Days*.[3] Hesiod was a peasant from a miserable village in Boeotia, although he had learned the minstrel's profession. He wrote for his fellows, giving them good counsel in regard to their occupation and their life. He passionately preaches labor, by which man earns his livelihood, and justice, which allows him to enjoy its fruits. It is interesting to see that the wisdom of Hesiod is often expressed in the same forms as the wisdom of the peasants of other nations. He has a like predilection for proverbs, maxims, and enigmatical expressions; for example, he calls the snail "he who carries his house." He takes notice of the stars, the migrating birds, and other indications of the change of the seasons.

It is not this, however, which is of interest in this connection, but his rules for the religious life and for the conduct of man, two things which for him are inseparable. There are in his writings expressions of a piety pervading the life of man such as is seldom found among the Greeks. He prescribes a prayer to Demeter and Zeus in the earth when the hand is laid to the plow to begin the autumn sowing, in order that the ears of corn may be full and heavy. This is a hallowing of labor which is not far from Protestant ideas. He prescribes the bringing of animal sacrifices to the gods in a chaste and pure manner according to each man's ability and

[3] Hesiod, *Works and Days,* ed. T. A. Sinclair (London, 1932).

the pouring out of libations and offering of frankincense in the morning when one rises and in the evening when one retires. This seems like ardent piety. But ritualism, which is only another name for legalism, is much more prominent in Hesiod. He gives rules for good behavior, mixed with religious rules. These are on a superstitious level, being characterized by a fear of offending gods or daemons. The words cited above, which testify to a genuine piety, are followed by a collection of maxims concerning intercourse with friends, neighbors, and relatives. At the end of the poem there is another collection of maxims beginning with more rules. You must not cross a river without praying while looking into its water, or without washing your hands, for the gods are angry with those who cross a river without washing away their wickedness and washing their hands. You must not take your food from a vessel which has not been consecrated. Ordinary rules of purity are numerous, for example the prohibition against pouring out a libation to Zeus with unwashed hands. There are also a number of superstitious rules, most of which are well known from modern folklore: you may not cut your nails at a sacrificial meal, a boy may not sit down on that which it is not permitted to move, a man may not bathe in a bath for women.

Such prescriptions occur elsewhere. They were especially taken up by the exoteric school of the Pythagoreans, the so-called *akousmatikoi*.[4] Pious and ritual and superstitious and merely secular rules of conduct are blended without any distinction. Especially interesting from our point of view is the addition to Hesiod's poem, which is properly called *The Days*. It is generally recognized that it was not composed by Hesiod himself, and this is probably true of the second collection of maxims also. But the date of composition is not

[4] See my forthcoming *Gesch. der griech. Rel.*, I, 665 ff.

much later, and from our point of view the diversity of authorship does not matter. On the contrary it is valuable because it proves that the same train of thought was common and that the same ideas were widely disseminated. *The Days* enumerates most of the days of the lunar month, though not all of them, and characterizes them in accordance with the maxim that a day is sometimes a mother, sometimes a stepmother. *The Days* prescribes on which days certain of the tasks of agriculture and stockbreeding should be performed and describes the significance of the days for family life and birth. It is very similar to the popular astrological predictions which are found in late antiquity, printed in handbooks (*Bauernpraktik*) and not yet completely forgotten. We do not include these things in religion. In late antiquity it was otherwise, for these predictions are part of astrology, which in that age was a dominant form of religion, culminating in sun worship. The calendar of lucky and unlucky days in Hesiod also belongs to a religious system, probably of Babylonian origin. Its religious importance is proved by the fact that certain days of the lunar month are designated as birthdays of the gods. Two such birthdays are mentioned in Hesiod.

About the same time the calendars of the Greek states were regulated, probably at the instigation of the Delphic oracle.[5] The eight year intercalary cycle was introduced, and the festivals were fixed on certain days of the lunar month. This regulation of the calendar is connected with the belief in the different virtues of the days of the lunar month, but there is a notable difference. Apollo paid attention to the cult of the gods only. The people wanted the guidance of religion in all matters, even those belonging to practical life. Apollo did not satisfy this demand. He cared only for the cult.

[5] See my "Entstehung und religiöse Bedeutung des griechischen Kalenders," *Lunds universitets årsskrift,* XIV: 2 (1918), No. 21.

According to our notions, much of this has little or nothing to do with religion, but all these rules are to a certain degree cognate. They are an outcome of legalism, of the endeavor to lay down definite prescriptions for all actions. In religion this is called ritualism, and ritualism, extended to the whole of human life, is a dominant factor in certain religions. But the Greek gods, fortunately for their people, did not care about the details of daily life, provided that the simple prescriptions of the cult were observed. Apollo required purity of hands, especially in regard to bloodguilt, and he did a great work in impressing upon the people a respect for human life. But the ritualism which Apollo promoted concerned cult, not daily life. Hesiod refers not to Apollo but to Zeus as the protector of his prescriptions. In Hesiod there appears a tendency towards a more severe kind of ritualism, such as is found among the Jews, fastening its fetters on the whole of man's life. But it was only a tendency, for the Greeks were too sensible to push legalism to the bitter end. It is, however, very interesting to see how strongly this tendency took hold of the people and how the representatives of religion, especially the Delphic oracle, saved it from these restraints, endorsing ritualism in cult only, not in daily life. The appeal of cultual ritualism was, however, so great in that age that Apollo at Delphi founded his dominant position upon it.

The tendency to legalism as well as to mysticism belongs to the early age before the Persian Wars. In the last century of this era social conditions began to improve. In politics the lead was taken by statesmen belonging to the middle class who wanted peace and quiet. In the sphere of religion they were supported by the Delphic oracle, the leading authority in religious matters. This oracle maintained the ancestral customs and the more orderly forms of cult and religion, and it was hostile to the excesses both of legalism and of mysticism. The representatives of this trend were the so-called Seven Sages, and their slogans, which were inscribed on the temple of Apollo at Delphi, were "Nothing too much" and "Know thyself," that is, know that thou art only a man. An Apolline piety was developed which taught the inferiority of man to the gods. Man must bow to the will of the gods and he must not be proud of his pious works and of his offerings to them.

A great change came about with the victory over the Persians. It was a victory of the Greek gods and heroes, that is of the Greek state religion. If we know the character of this religion, of which I have spoken earlier, we know that the consequence was the still further repression of the mystical and legalistic movements which had sprung from the depths of the popular mind.

Another dominant issue in the early age was the problem of justice. Although its greatest importance lay on the social plane, it influenced religion also in many respects. I cannot expatiate on this here. I will only make the following brief remarks. From of old, Zeus was the protector of justice, and he is celebrated as such by Hesiod, Aeschylus, and many others. But he was a theoretical more than a practical protector. His rule was too arbitrary to allow him to appear as a true guardian of justice, and the same was true of the behavior of the Greek gods in general. The demand for social justice was a demand for the equalization of social rights. One of its motives was a very human envy of the rich and mighty. It found an argument in the vicissitudes of human life. The higher a man rose, the greater was his fall. This was proved by the fate of many men, not to speak of the tyrants. So the conception of the *hybris* of man and the *nemesis* of the gods came into existence. The translations "wantonness" and "jealousy" do not quite hit the mark. Hybris is the feeling of being supported by good luck, nemesis is the feeling of something unjust, improper. The idea of hybris and the corresponding idea of nemesis are akin to the slogan "Know thyself." Both teach man the humble position which befits him.

These ideas are very often found in literature, and it may be asked how far they belonged not only to the educated classes but also to the people. The people demanded justice, but the battle for justice was fought on the social rather than on the religious plane. The conceptions of hybris and nemesis had a popular background in what the Greeks called *baskania*, the belief, still common in southern Europe, that excessive praise is dangerous and a cause of misfortune. Even we are accustomed to saying "touch wood" if things go exceptionally well with us. It was customary, and is so still, to avert such a danger by spitting into one's bosom or by making an obscene gesture. The impressive scene in the *Agamemnon* of Aeschylus, in which the king fears to tread on purple carpets when entering his palace lest the envy of some evil eye should harm him, is taken from real life.[6] Herodotus' story of the tyrant Polycrates contains a folk-tale motif which is still current.[7] When King Amasis heard of Polycrates' exceptional good luck he advised him to offset it by throwing away something which he valued very highly. Polycrates obeyed and threw a costly ring into the sea, but it was found again in the stomach of a fish which was brought to him a few days later by a fisherman. When Amasis heard this he renounced so dangerous a friendship, and Polycrates ended his life on the cross. This belief was popular, but it may be doubted if it was religious in the true sense of the

---

[6] *Agamemnon,* vss. 945 ff.
[7] Herodotus, III, 40 ff.

word. Fate is the work of the gods; but in Herodotus, at least, this is never said of a specific god, but always of "the gods" collectively or of "the divine" in the abstract. The belief comes very near to fatalism. It is a kind of philosophy of life and its vicissitudes rather than a religious conception.

I remarked that certain kinds of legalism come very near to superstition and that Hesiod has prescriptions which are also current in modern folklore. We are accustomed to making a clear-cut distinction between religion and superstition. Superstition is something which is not allowed in a Christian and which is unworthy of him. The situation was somewhat different in ancient Greece. The Greek word which we usually translate by "superstition" is *deisidaimonia*, fear of the *daimones*. But these include the gods also, as in Homer and elsewhere. Consequently the word can and sometimes must be translated "fear of the gods." Xenophon still uses it in this good sense when he praises King Agesilaus for his deisidaimonia, his reverence for the gods.[8] In Theophrastus' characterization of the *deisidaimon*[9] the sense has deteriorated and the word can rightly be translated by "superstition." The superstitious man is one who, if something happens, washes his hands, sprinkles himself with holy water, and walks about the whole day with laurel leaves in his mouth. If a weasel crosses his path, he waits for another person walking the same way or he throws three stones over the road. If he sees a snake in his house, he invokes Sabazios if it is a *pareias*. If it is a so-called holy snake, he erects a hero shrine on the place. He pours out oil on the stones at the crossroads when he passes and, falling on his knees, he venerates them before he continues on his way. If a mouse has gnawed a hole in his flour sack, he goes to the exegete and asks what

[8] *Agesilaus,* XI, 8.
[9] *Characteres,* 16.

to do. If the exegete replies that he is to give it to the leatherworker to be repaired, he does not listen to him but turns away and carries out purifications and the like. We see that popular superstitions and the purificatory customs of the common religion were mixed up, and from the last sentence quoted it appears that official representatives of religion treated such exaggerated fears humorously. In ancient Greece the difference between religion and superstition was a difference of degree rather than of kind. There were also merely popular superstitions, but even these were not sharply distinguishable from certain religious ideas.

The general opinion is that the Greeks of the classical age were happily free from superstition. I am sorry that I am obliged to refute this opinion. There was a great deal of superstition in Greece, even when Greek culture was at its height and even in the center of that culture, Athens. Superstition is very seldom mentioned in the literature of the period simply because great writers found such base things not worth mentioning. But the Greeks borrowed Hecate from Caria because they needed a goddess of witchcraft and ghosts, and in the classical age her triple image was erected before every house in order to avert evils of that kind. Aristophanes is a witness to the fact that witchcraft was well known.[10] He makes Strepsiades say that he wants to buy a Thessalian witch to bring down the moon and shut it up, and he mentions necromantics, the calling up of the dead to foretell the future, a kind of mantic which was almost completely absent from Greece in early times.

Very important is the tract on the holy disease, that is, epilepsy. It is one of the earliest in the collection ascribed to Hippocrates,[11] and was probably written by him. At any

---

[10] *Nubes,* vss. 749 ff., and *Aves,* vss. 1553 ff.
[11] *De morbo sacro,* 1.

rate it belongs to the fifth century B.C. It should be read by everyone who wants to become acquainted with the religious situation of the time. The author says that the men who call this disease holy are of the same kind as the magicians, charlatans, and purificatory and begging priests and that they cover up their ignorance and helplessness by the pretext that this disease is holy. They resort to purifications and spells. They prescribe the avoidance of black garments and of putting one foot on another or one hand on another. These are the methods of magic, well known from folklore. The author further tells us that some people pretended to be able by certain secret rites to bring down the moon, eclipse the sun, cause storm or calm, bring rain or drought, call forth water, or make the earth sterile. He includes a catalogue of magical achievements of the sort described in the Roman age and generally believed to belong to that age only. As a matter of fact they were much older, although they were more in evidence at a later time, when the soberness of the old religion had vanished. Our author informs us that these people had drawn the gods also into the circle of their superstitious ideas. If the sick man bellows or has convulsions, they say that the Great Mother is responsible. If his cries resemble neighing, Poseidon is the cause; if they resemble the chirping of birds, Apollo Nomios is to blame; and if he foams at the mouth and kicks with his feet, it is Ares' doing. Finally, if he has evil dreams by night, sees frightful figures, and leaps up from his bed, they say that he has been attacked by Hecate or by some hero.

The last words call for some comment. Ghost stories like those current even in our day were current in antiquity also. In literature they do not appear until the Roman age. Their apparent absence in the classical age is deceptive. Ghosts went by the name of heroes, and genuine ghost stories are related of the heroes. I have mentioned the hero of Temesa, to whom the inhabitants were compelled to sacrifice yearly the fairest virgin of their town until a well-known pugilist by the sheer force of his fists drove him into the sea, and Orestes, whom no Athenian liked to meet by night because he was likely to give him a thrashing and to rob him of his clothes. There was also Actaeon, who devastated the fields of the Boeotians until on the advice of the oracle his statue was chained to a rock. Plautus' comedy *Mostellaria*, which was copied from the Greek poet Philemon, is a ghost story of a very common type. A guest-friend has been killed and buried in a certain house. He walks about at night, disquieting and frightening people, so that nobody dares to live in the haunted house.

The account in Hippocrates concerns disease, and in cases where human resources fail superstition flourishes strongly even in our day. Even Pericles, who was above such base things, had to tolerate the tying of an amulet to him by the women when he was ill.[12] Of the cures in the Asclepieion at Epidaurus, the most miraculous and unbelievable tales are related.[13] I will not enter into the sane and sober views of Hippocrates on religion, although they are worth reading. I turn instead to another author who has much to say about magic and magicians, Plato. He prescribes the severest punishments for men who pretend to be able to call up the dead; to coerce the gods through the magical powers of sacrifices, prayers, and spells; and to destroy individuals, whole families, and towns. He speaks of several tricks, spells, and imprecations of black magic and of wax dolls which

[12] Plutarch, *Pericles*, 38.

[13] The inscriptions are collected in *Inscriptiones Graecae,* Editio minor, Vol. IV, Fasc. 1, Nos. 121-27. See also R. Herzog, "Die Wunderheilungen von Epidauros," *Philologus,* Supplementary Vol. XXII(1931), No. 3.

are seen at doors, at crossroads, and on tombs.[14] It is a well-known fact, and one frequently mentioned in a later age, that witches and sorcerers used dolls for their purposes, burning them, transfixing them, and so forth, in order to affect with like pain the persons whom they represented. Plato's description is much more suggestive of the witchcraft of late antiquity than of the fourth century B.C., but it is impossible to doubt that he took it from the life of his own times.

This can be corroborated. When Plato speaks of imprecations he uses the word *katadeseis*. These are leaden tablets inscribed with imprecations directed against persons named on them and deposited in tombs in order to devote these cursed persons to the gods of the nether world. A great number of these *tabellae defixionis* have been found and published,[15] but it has been too little remarked that many of them belong to the fourth century B.C. A curious unpublished inscription on the shard of a cup, which reads "I put quartan fever on Aristion to the death," is probably as early as the end of the fifth century B.C. Numerous leaden tablets have been found at Athens, and it is a very interesting and important fact that many of the names mentioned on them are names of historically known persons. We find two brothers of the well-known politician Callistratus, who was exiled in 361 B.C.; Callias and Hipponicus, from the wealthy and famous house of the *dadouchoi*; Demophilus, the prosecutor of Aristotle and Phocion; Demosthenes; Lycurgus; and other orators and politicians. This is astonishing. The names mentioned show that belief in the magical power of these imprecations was not confined to artisans, hawkers, and such

---

[14] *Laws,* X, p. 909b; see also p. 908d and XI, p. 933.
[15] The Attic *tabellae defixionis* have been published by R. Wünsch in an appendix to *Inscriptiones Graecae,* III. Several important finds have appeared later. See my forthcoming *Gesch. der griech. Rel.,* I, 757 ff.

people, who also appear among those cursed. It must have been current even in the best society.

Most of these curses refer to lawsuits. The gods, especially Hecate and Hermes of the nether world, are asked to tie the soul, the intellect, the tongue, and the limbs of the person cursed. It is manifest that these imprecations are connected with the degeneration of the Athenian democracy and law courts and with the abuses and cavils of the sycophants. I am obliged to state, although I am very sorry to do it, that superstition and a belief in magic and witchcraft were very common and widespread in the heyday of the classical age. If this was so in Athens, it can hardly have been less so in backward districts of Greece. Furthermore, it must be acknowledged that this recrudescence of superstition and magic is connected with the decay of the old religion, which was secularized by the state and attacked by the Sophists. When such a void is created in religion, the opportunity is present for the flourishing of superstition and magic and the immigration of new gods.

The leaden tablets with imprecations were deposited in tombs, a sure sign of the belief in the power of the dead to do harm. Belief in the power of the dead appears in the old tomb cult. It was supposed to belong to the individual who was buried in the tomb and venerated there, and who was called up to help his family. Our notions of the cult of the dead are derived from literature, especially from the tragedies, which cling to what is old. The cult of the dead had, however, been suppressed for political and social reasons and had lost much of its vigor. The belief in ghosts remained. The general Greek idea of the other world was of something else, the dark and gloomy Hades with its pale, dumb, powerless shadows. It was so ingrained in the Greek mind that, in spite of the fact that Christianity has preached quite a different conception for nearly two thousand years, the nether world of the Greek peasant is the same today. Its lord has kept the name of the ancient ferryman, Charon or Charos, although he is represented as a horseman and hunter. The shadows were powerless. They were supposed to have the same appearance which the man had during his life or at the moment of his death. Odysseus recognizes his deceased comrades in Hades. This is constantly so among all peoples. The life of this world is the pattern after which the other life is pictured, although the shadows may be darker or lighter. There is one exemption from the gloominess of Hades, the bliss awaiting those initiated in the Eleusinian Mysteries. But even this consists in a repetition of the celebration of the Mysteries, and nothing was required for it but initiation.

While for Homer the body is the man himself and the soul is a pale shadow worth nothing, the Orphics considered the soul as immortal and the body as its prison.[16] The soul was able to leave the body temporarily in dreams and left it once for all in death. The consequence of this doctrine was a new evaluation of the other life. For the Orphics, also, initiation and the accompanying purification were necessary, but they added a demand for righteousness and moral purity. He who has not been purified in this life will continue in his impurity in the other life. "He will lie in the mud" is the keynote of the new ideas of the other world. There is here a recurrence of the old idea of the repetition of this life, modified only in so far as the repetition in itself is regarded as a punishment. This is not infrequently the case in modern folklore.

The Orphic idea is expressed in certain myths, including that of the Danaids. The figures which are generally called Danaids were represented in the picture by Polygnotus at Del-

[16] Plato, *Cratylus,* p. 400c.

phi as those who had not been initiated and who were compelled in the other life to carry water for their purification, unceasingly and in vain. If the idea took hold on the popular mind, this was because it was coupled with another idea dear to the Greeks, that of retributive justice. In early times the individual was only a link in the chain of the family. Children and children's children had to pay for the trespasses of their ancestors. There came a time when it seemed unjust that one individual should pay for the trespasses of another. It was demanded that the man who had trespassed should be punished, that he himself and no other should pay for his guilt. We find this demand in Solon. But experience taught that a man who had committed unjust deeds sometimes died without having suffered the fitting punishment. The solution of the dilemma was found in the Orphic doctrine. The punishment due was transferred to the life after death.

Sinners punished in the underworld, such as Tantalus and Sisyphus, are familiar from mythology. Originally they were enemies of the gods who were punished by the gods in the upper world, and only later were they transferred to the underworld. This underworld is described in the eleventh book of the *Odyssey*, and it was depicted by the great painter Polygnotus in a famous picture at Delphi.[17] But this picture contained something new. It represented a man who, having killed his father, was strangled by him, and a man who, having robbed a temple, was punished by a woman in various ways. Punishments were invented in accordance with the old *jus talionis*, an eye for an eye and a tooth for a tooth, or were taken from human justice. This idea of punishment in the other world was fatally extended, and occasions were found for the invention and addition of ever new modes of torture

[17] Described by Pausanias, X, 28 ff.

and punishment. The driving force was the idea of retributive justice.

Before long the underworld was pictured as a place of horror, a hell in the full sense of the word. Aristophanes describes it in *The Frogs*. He fills it with frightful beasts, snakes, and monsters like Empousa. There in the mud and ever-flowing mire lie those who have committed wrongs to guest-friends, frauds, or perjury or who have beaten their fathers. Aristophanes also gives a detailed enumeration of the most frightful pains which can be inflicted upon a man, copied from the mythological punishments, and enlarged upon and extended in a grotesque manner.

All this is known well enough, but it is generally set aside on the ground that it is mythology and has as little importance for real belief as myths ordinarily have. But it had a very serious background. Aristophanes would not have been able to give such a long and picturesque description of hell and its horrors if the subject had not been familiar to his audience. Elsewhere in literature such things are not mentioned. Like superstition, they were too base and grotesque. But there are two exceptions, two very important passages which prove beyond doubt that the idea of punishment in the other world had taken strong hold on the popular mind in the fifth and fourth centuries B.C. The philosopher Democritus says: "Many people who do not know that human nature is dissolved in death, but who know that they have committed much wrong, live constantly in fear and anxiety, composing lying fables concerning the time after death."[18] And in the introduction to his great work the *Republic*, Plato makes the aged Kephalos say that a man who sees the hour of death approaching is seized by fright and begins to think about

[18] Frag. 297, in H. Diels, *Die Fragmente der Vorsokratiker,* 5th ed. (Berlin, 1934-37), II, 206-7.

things that had not troubled him before. For while the myths that are told of the underworld, according to which he who has committed wrongs in this world will be punished in that world, seemed ridiculous to him hitherto, now his soul is anxious, for they may be true. He is disquieted and he makes up his account, considering whether he has done wrong to anybody. If he finds that he has committed many unjust actions, he is filled with alarm; he often leaps up from his bed in sleep as children do, and he lives in fear.[19] This is a striking picture and drawn from life. Plato's own detailed accounts of the other world and of metempsychosis must be passed over here, for they are myths created by him and have nothing to do with popular ideas. Their influence on the future, however, was great and fateful.

A reference may be added to the paintings of the Apulian tomb vases, which belong to the fourth century B.C. and are an offshoot of Attic vase painting. They represent the palace of Hades and the mythological criminals punished in the underworld. That such subjects were chosen for tomb monuments proves that these ideas were popular in southern Italy. This is, perhaps, especially due to the strong Orphic influence in that country.

Long ago Dieterich tried to prove that hell was created by the Greeks.[20] Another great scholar, Cumont, has, on the contrary, derived it from the Orient.[21] But if we take the earliest Christian vision of hell, the so-called Apocalypse of St. Peter, which was the starting point of Dieterich's research, it appears that Dieterich was right. The description of the punishments for moral sins, which were sins for the heathens also,

---

[19] Plato, *Republic,* I, pp. 330d ff.

[20] A. Dieterich, *Nekyia; Beiträge zur Erklärung der neuentdeckten Petrusapokalypse* (Leipzig, 1893; 2d ed., 1913).

[21] F. Cumont, *After Life in Roman Paganism* (New Haven, 1922), pp. 88 ff.

is detailed, and the old keynote, the lying in the mud, recurs constantly in many variations. On the other hand, the description of the punishments of unbelievers is briefer, less detailed, and evidently copied from the former. The background is Greek.

I have dwelt here on the dark and base sides of Greek religion—superstition, magic, and the idea of punishment in the other world. For I am of the opinion that it is necessary to know these also if we are to have a true conception of Greek popular religion. We know that such ideas became dominant in late antiquity. The way was prepared by the decay of the old religion. Man needs some kind of religion. If his old faith is destroyed, he turns to superstition and magic and to new gods who are imported from foreign countries or who rise from the dark depths of the human mind. There were such depths in the Greek mind also. That mind was not so exclusively bright as is sometimes said.

SEERS AND ORACLES

THE RELIGIOUS SITUATION IN GREECE WAS COMPLICATED in the fifth and fourth centuries B.C., even in regard to popular religion. It was simple enough in backward districts, where the old faith survived without being disturbed and where the people kept the rustic customs, celebrated the old festivals, and venerated the gods and heroes without doing much thinking about the high gods. The background of this simple faith has survived until our own day. The situation was different elsewhere, especially in the cities, where religion had to encounter political life and the new enlightenment. The people ascribed the greatness and glory of the state, its freedom and independence, to its great gods; they feasted gladly on the sacrifices offered by the state; and they gathered with others at the panegyreis. But the cult of the great gods was too cold. These gods did not offer help in human needs and consolation to a contrite heart. The old bonds of state and family were loosened, the individual became conscious of himself. The state claimed as great authority as ever, but, as a matter of fact, the abuses of democracy turned people away from it and made them try to find the way that pleased them best. Man was no longer born to his gods as in earlier times. He wanted to find his gods for himself. And so he turned to gods who could help him—to Asclepius, the great healer of diseases; to the Cabiri, who brought help in distress at sea; or to gods who were able to stir his religious feelings deeply, as Sabazios could. In this movement the women seem to have played an

important part. The criticism of religious beliefs by the Sophists and the improper jests at the expense of the gods by men
like Aristophanes did their work. Atheists were not unknown,
nor were statesmen who treated religion as only a means to
their ends. The faith of the masses was shaken, but it was
not destroyed.

On occasion it broke out violently, and the people were
seized by a kind of religious hysteria when they believed that
their welfare and that of their city was threatened by impiety
against the gods. The Athenian trials for impiety are famous.[1]
The trials of Pericles' mistress, Aspasia, and of his friend,
the philosopher Anaxagoras, had a very obvious political
background. This is apparent also in the trial of Alcibiades
for profanation of the Eleusinian Mysteries and in the famous
trial for the smashing of the herms in 415 B.C. On this occasion a real religious hysteria broke out, for these events took
place just before the great fleet sailed for Syracuse. The
people feared that the wrath of the gods would imperil this
great and dangerous undertaking, or at least they found an
evil omen in the event. About the same time the Sophist
Protagoras and the atheist Diagoras were condemned for
impiety. Most famous of all is the trial and death of Socrates.
Socrates was accused of seducing youths and of not having
the same gods as the state but other new gods. His accusers
were good citizens who tried to heal the terrible wounds left
by the war and by the terrorism of the Thirty Tyrants, and
they sincerely believed that they would attain their goal by
removing the adversary of the old faith and old customs.
They made a tragic mistake, for they struck at the man who
overcame the sophistical criticism. Such trials also took place
later. Even Aristotle was threatened with one.

[1] E. Derenne, *Les Procès d'impiété intentés aux philosophes à Athènes au
Vme et au IVme siècles avant J.-C.* (Liége, 1930).

Except in the case of the simple rustic cults, it was the fate of Greek religion to be closely interconnected with political life. We should remember that the people of whose religion we speak made up the popular assembly and that the assembly made decisions in religious matters, even if in such matters it acknowledged a superior authority and asked the Delphic or some other oracle for advice. This intermingling of religion and politics is especially apparent in another field of religion which was of the greatest importance in practical life. I refer to the foretelling of the future. We can hardly imagine how great its importance was in private as well as in public life. In my opinion it was the part of religion which was of most current interest in that age.

The cities asked the oracles for advice not only in religious but also in other matters, and private persons did so on all occasions of any importance. Furthermore, guidance was sought from sacrifices, birds, dreams, and other omens. We may take Xenophon as an example. He was a brave and well-educated man, a skilled officer, and a good writer, but without philosophical understanding. His religious views were certainly those of the Athenian middle class. He turned to oracles and seers on all occasions. Before Xenophon went to Asia Minor to join the expedition of Cyrus he asked the Delphic oracle to which gods he should sacrifice in order that he might make the voyage and return in safety.[2] When the Army of the Ten Thousand was at discord, he sacrificed and asked the gods if he should go back home. He did likewise when the chief command was offered to him and when he was thinking of settling the soldiers at Kotyora.[3] He firmly believed he was led by presages and omens. A dream in which he saw a thunderbolt strike his father's house was the immediate cause

---

[2] *Anabasis,* III, 1, 5 ff.
[3] *Ibid.,* V, 6, 16 ff.

of his assembling the officers after the death of Cyrus in order
to take counsel in the difficult situation of the army. A dream
showed him the means of crossing the river Tigris when the
army seemed to be cut off by the river and the mountains.[4]
When he was riding from Ephesus in order to meet Cyrus, he
heard the cry of a seated eagle to the right, and the seer who
accompanied him said that it signified glory but many hardships.[5] And, finally, when someone sneezed during an exhorta-
tory speech to the soldiers after the murder of Clearchus, all
the soldiers venerated the gods.[6] Xenophon firmly believed in
presages, and when they seemed to fail he took pains to explain
that they finally proved to be true. I hardly need to refer to
the many oracles and presages related by Herodotus.

The wish to be able to cast a glance into the future is common
to all humanity. Even in our day there are plenty of soothsay-
ers and sibyls, and many people still believe in dreams and
omens. It is no wonder that the ancients did so, too. But we
should keep well in mind that while these arts are now despised
by educated people and ranked with superstition they were an
acknowledged part of Greek religion. The great popularity
of the Delphic oracle was based on its supposed ability to
foretell the future. There were numerous oracles in Greece,
and, to judge from Herodotus, they seem especially to have
flourished before and during the Persian Wars. But they were
consulted eagerly in the following age too, although a certain
decline in their prestige is perhaps to be found in the fact that
at this time the Greeks turned to foreign oracles, especially
that of Ammon in the Great Oasis. In the Hellenistic age the
old oracles of Greece lost their popularity.

The writers preserve only the more important questions put

[4] *Ibid.*, III, 1, 11 ff.; see also VI, 1, 22, and IV, 3, 8 ff.
[5] *Ibid.*, VI, 1, 23.
[6] *Ibid.*, III, 2, 9.

to the oracles. We can be certain that people applied to the oracles on all occasions which were of some importance to them. But these questions pertaining to ordinary life are lost, with one exception. At Dodona there have been found several leaden tablets inscribed with questions which people asked the oracle.[7] It is interesting to see what they were like. One Heraclides asks whether his wife will bear him a child, and Lysanias asks whether the child with which Amyla is pregnant is his. One man asks if it will be profitable for him to buy a house and land in the town, another if he will do well by breeding sheep, a third if he will make a profit by carrying goods around and doing business where he likes. We see what sort of advice people wanted in family life and business, and we can understand the important part which the oracles played in practical life. We should not forget that other omens and dreams were eagerly observed also.

Whoever has read the accounts of Greek historians knows that no battle was waged, no river crossed, before victims had been slaughtered and the signs of the sacrifice were favorable. If the signs were unfavorable a second and even a third victim were slaughtered until favorable signs appeared, and it sometimes happened that a general held his army back and waited for favorable signs even when the enemy had already begun to attack. It sometimes happened also that a plan was given up if the signs were unfavorable. Seers always accompanied the armies; among the Ten Thousand there were several of them.

To us it seems paradoxical to wait for sacrificial omens before a battle when quick action is required or before a march which is demanded by strategical considerations. The Greeks thought otherwise, or they would have abolished these hindrances to military action. We should not overlook the psychological influence of these god-sent signs on the soldiers and

[7] C. Carapanos, *Dodone et ses ruines* (Paris, 1878), pp. 68 ff.

on their conduct in battle, for the soldiers believed in the
signs as Xenophon did. Of course there were cunning seers
who interpreted the signs from the victim sacrificed in accordance with military necessity, and there were generals who
imposed their will upon the seers and used these sacrifices
as a means to their military ends. In the battle at Plataea,
Pausanias held his soldiers back, under the pretext that the
signs were unfavorable, until the enemy could be attacked by
the hoplites at a reasonable distance. But there were also
bigoted generals who obeyed the seers rather than military
necessity. The most tragic example is Nicias and the defeat
of the Athenians before Syracuse. When the retreat was de-
cided on the moon was eclipsed, and the seers interpreted this
to mean that the army had to remain on the spot thrice nine
days. Nicias obeyed, and the delay sealed their doom.[8] In his
biography of Nicias, Plutarch deplores the untimely death of
the seer Stilbides because after that no wise seer was at the
side of Nicias.[9]

There were seers who intrigued on their own account. The
seer Silanos, who was asked by Xenophon to consult the gods
in regard to his plan to settle the soldiers at Kotyora, frustrated his intention because he wanted to go back to Greece.[10]
In a military writer of the same age there is a very instructive
prescription to the effect that a general should have a strict
eye upon the seers during a siege and not allow them to sacrifice on their own account in the absence of the general.[11] They
might have a fatal influence on public opinion.

The part played by the seers in war may seem to be of a
special kind, but wars were only too common in Greece. Between the great and historically famous wars some small war

[8] Thucydides, VII, 50.
[9] *Nicias*, 23.
[10] Xenophon, *Anabasis*, V, 6, 29.
[11] Aeneas Tacticus, *Poliorcetica*, 10, 4.

was almost always going on in some corner of the country. The gods were constantly consulted in time of war for the sake of the psychological effect on the minds of the combatants. From the account in Xenophon of the events in Troas,[12] it seems that seers circulated everywhere and offered their services to those who wanted and paid for them. It is striking that the seers whom he mentions were from backward provinces of Greece—Arcadia and Acarnania. Belief in the art was perhaps firmer in these regions. Some seers acquired a great fame. One of these was Tisamenus, who belonged to a famous family of seers from Olympia, the Iamidae,[13] and served as a seer in the great battles fought with the Persians. He even acquired Spartan citizenship.

If the seers were able to influence the minds of men in war, they, of course, had the same power in peace and in political life. Still more important were, however, the numerous oracle mongers, the *chresmologoi,* who circulated among the people oracles which were anonymous or which were ascribed to some old prophet, such as Musaeus or Bacis, or to some oracle. These oracles were not signs given by the gods in sacrifices or in other ways, but words—verses which the people learned by heart and which went from mouth to mouth. I hardly need to remark what a powerful means this was for influencing public opinion when an important decision was pending. But the part played by oracles and seers in such matters is not sufficiently appreciated, and so I must dwell upon it at some length. The oracles played a part in political agitation similar to that of newspapers and political pamphlets in our own times. Examples of their fateful influence will be given below.

This role of the oracles began before the Persian Wars.

---

[12] *Anabasis,* VII, 8.
[13] L. Weniger, "Die Seher von Olympia," *Archiv für Religionswissenschaft,* XVIII (1915), 53 ff.

Herodotus relates that when the Spartan king Cleomenes in 510 B.C. drove out the sons of Pisistratus and took the Acropolis of Athens, he seized in the temple a collection of oracles which had belonged to the Pisistratidae.[14] These oracles foretold many heavy blows that would be dealt by the Athenians to the Spartans. In this connection I may also recall the fact that the political adversaries of the Pisistratidae, the Alcmaeonidae, whom they had exiled, secured the help of the Delphic oracle and through it of the Spartans. What had happened is clear enough. The Pisistratidae knew that the Spartans were their most powerful enemies, and they collected these oracles not for their own pleasure but in order to prepare the minds of the people for the war with the Spartans which they foresaw—to exhort the people and to give them courage in the fight with the formidable foe.

Another story is told by Herodotus about Onomacritus, who is known chiefly because he seems to have promoted Orphism. He was exiled by Hipparchus, the son of Pisistratus, because another poet, Lasus of Hermione, had caught him falsely inserting into a collection of oracles ascribed to Musaeus an oracle prophesying that the islands around Lemnos would be engulfed by the sea. I do not think that the real reason for the exile was that Onomacritus had committed a literary forgery. If we recall that Lemnos was occupied by Miltiades about 512 B.C., certainly not without the consent of the Pisistratidae, and that it afforded support to the commercial and political influence of Athens in the northeastern part of the Aegean for which the Pisistratidae cared much (I recall that they seized Sigeum at the mouth of the Hellespont), the political background becomes clear. Such an oracle was unfavorable to their political plans. After his exile Onomacritus went to the court of the Persian king, where he used his

14 Herodotus, V, 90.

oracles in order to persuade the king to undertake the campaign against Greece. He read a mass of oracles, and if something was unfavorable to the Persians, he concealed it, picking out the most favorable oracles.[15] We see what oracles were good for.

There were many such collections of oracles, and their authority was enhanced by ascribing them to some famous old prophet. The most esteemed of these was Bacis. Herodotus quotes oracles at length only from him and from the Pythia. In one passage he makes an interesting remark which proves that criticism had begun to awaken. Speaking of a notorious *ex eventu* oracle referring to the battle at Artemisium, Herodotus says that he is unable to deny that oracles are true and that, as Bacis speaks so clearly, he is not willing to put forward or to tolerate any contradiction in this regard.[16] The home of the Sibyl was not in Greece but in Asia Minor. Another collection ascribed to her was brought from the Greek colony of Cumae to Rome at about the same time. It is the famous *Sibylline Books*. A Sibylline oracle ascribed to 125 B.C. is preserved in Phlegon.[17] It is certainly not genuine. We need only remark that it consists chiefly of prescriptions for sacrifices and purifications, though it also contains certain political allusions. In judging the much discussed problem of the *Sibylline Books,* it is important to realize that it was only one of the many collections of oracles circulating in Greece at the

[15] Herodotus, VII, 6. See also H. Diels, "Über Epimenides von Kreta," *Sitzungsberichte der Königlich preussischen Akademie der Wissenschaften* (Berlin), 1891, pp. 396 ff., and H. Bengtson, "Einzelpersönlichkeit und athenischer Staat zur Zeit des Peisistratos und des Miltiades," *Sitzungsberichte der Bayerischen Akademie der Wissenschaften, Philos.-hist. Abt.* (Munich), 1939, No. 1, pp. 26 ff.

[16] Herodotus, VIII, 77.

[17] The text is printed in H. Diels, *Sibyllinische Blätter* (Berlin, 1890), pp. 111 ff.

end of the sixth century B.C. Of course, such collections circulated also in the Greek colonies.

Thucydides gives an illuminating account of the role of the oracles during the Peloponnesian War. He is a child of the enlightenment of the age of the Sophists and does not believe in them. He mentions them only in order to show their psychological influence and the impression they made on men's minds. It was of course a great advantage for the Spartans that when they asked Apollo at Delphi about the war he declared that they would conquer and that he would help them whether called upon or not. This increased the willingness of Sparta's allies to take part in the war. But this was also an example of the oracle's interference in politics which ended by depriving it of its authority. When the great plague broke out during the first years of the war, there was an animated discussion in regard to the true wording of an old oracle. Should it read: "The Dorian war will come and with it famine (*limos*)"? Or should the last word be "plague" (*loimos*)? An oracle of Pythia prohibited people from settling in the Pelargikon on the southern slope of the Acropolis. As this was necessarily done when the country was evacuated and the people crowded into the town, many thought that this infringement of the divine prohibition was the cause of the calamities. Thucydides remarks dryly that, on the contrary, the calamity of the war was the reason why the Pelargikon was inhabited. When the Spartans invaded Attica for the first time and devastated the fields, the Athenians were at discord as to whether they should go and fight the enemy, and the oracle mongers proffered numerous oracles which all were eager to hear.[18]

The most outstanding and flagrant example of the role of oracles and seers in political discussions and of their use to influence public opinion occurred in the preparation for the

[18] Thucydides, II, 54, 17, 21.

expedition to Sicily. The undertaking was hotly disputed. There were two parties, one of which found the risk too great and rejected the proposal, while the other adhered to it ardently. The leader of the party favoring the expedition was Alcibiades, whose motives were selfish. Whatever he thought of it, he promoted the plan in order to win glory and power for himself. It was all important for him to control public opinion. He had a seer who prophesied that the Athenians would earn great glory in Sicily. His adversaries and even priests used the same methods. An embassy sent to the oracle of Ammon in the Great Oasis came back with the answer that the Athenians would take all Syracusans. Unfavorable sayings were concealed.[19] One of these oracles, one which came from Dodona, is preserved, together with the interpretation given after the catastrophe.[20] It said that the Athenians would settle on Sikelia. According to the interpretation, the oracle meant a small hill with this name outside the gates of Athens. Thucydides relates that after the great catastrophe the wrath of the people turned not only against the politicians but also against the oracle mongers and seers who, pretending divine inspiration, had raised false hopes in them.[21]

Plutarch relates several terrible omens which foreboded the catastrophe, beginning with the smashing of the herms and ending with the women's lament for Adonis about the time when the fleet sailed for Sicily. A man leaped up on the altar of the twelve gods and castrated himself. Ravens picked off a large part of a votive gift which the Athenians had erected at Delphi in memory of their victory over the Persians, a Palladium standing on a date palm of bronze. When, on the advice of the oracle, the Athenians fetched a priestess of

[19] Plutarch, *Nicias*, 13.
[20] Pausanias, VIII, 11, 12.
[21] Thucydides, VIII, 1.

Athena from Clazomenae, it turned out that her name was Hesychia (quiet). These stories may have been invented after the terrible end of the expedition, but at all events they are characteristic of the mentality of the age, the search for presages and omens everywhere and the great attention paid to them. Of course, the exegetes were asked to interpret them. The importance of seers, oracles, presages, omens, and the like for the popular mind will, I hope, be evident from these examples.

Seers and oracle mongers were omnipresent. Aristophanes is illuminating in this respect. In his comedy *The Birds*, when the City of the Birds in the Clouds is founded, among the charlatans who present themselves is an oracle monger who reads beautiful oracles from his book. He is chased away by Peisthetairos with another oracle. The intrigue in Aristophanes' comedy *The Knights* is a regular battle for the favor of old Demos, the personification of the Athenian people, fought by means of oracle collections. Cleon, the leading politician of this time, is represented as a Paphlagonian slave who has ousted the two other slaves of Demos, Nicias and Demosthenes, the two well-known generals. Cleon feeds the old Demos with oracles and wins his favor. The other two steal his book. In it they find an oracle saying that the leather-seller, that is, the tanner Cleon, will be vanquished by a sausage-seller, who is still more impudent than he. The sausage-seller is sought and found, and now the battle begins. The sausage-seller carries the day because his oracles promise much more to Demos. It is a bold joke, but it has a very serious background and throws light on the means by which the opinions of the people and of the popular assembly were influenced. Evidently seers and oracle mongers had the ear of the people and helped to determine the direction of public opinion.

Many of the seers, oracle mongers, and interpreters of

dreams, presages, and omens were charlatans. But they were not all so contemptible as they are represented by Aristophanes and as moderns are apt to think. Some of them were influential politicians, and among them were the exegetes, the official interpreters of sacred law chosen by the people and the Delphic oracle. The most prominent of these was Lampon, who was a very well-known personage in the latter part of the fifth century B.C. He took a prominent part in the founding of the Athenian colony Thurii, and a decree preserved in an inscription proves that he moved proposals in the popular assembly concerning sacred matters.[22] He was one of the official exegetes. Together with Lampon is mentioned Hierocles. Aristophanes derides Hierocles as an oracle monger, but the people commissioned him to arrange certain sacrifices for Euboea which were prescribed by the oracle and perhaps gave him a plot of land on Euboea.[23] We shall later mention Diopeithes, a friend of Nicias, whom Aristophanes calls avaricious in one passage and a great man in another.[24] He had a namesake at Sparta who must have been a person of consequence, for in the contest over the throne between Agesilaus and Leotychides he produced an oracle of Apollo directing the Spartans to beware of a lame kingship. Agesilaus had a lame leg. But the cunning Lysander outdid the Spartan Diopeithes, saying that the oracle referred to the illegitimate birth of Leotychides, for there was a rumor that he was the son not of King Agis but of Alcibiades.[25]

By virtue of their profession these men were the defenders of the old religion when Sophists and unbelievers directed their attacks against it. The trials for atheism were initiated

[22] Aristophanes, *Nubes,* vs. 332 and scholion; *Inscriptiones Graecae,* Editio minor, Vol. I, No. 76.
[23] Aristophanes, *Pax,* vss. 1046 ff., and scholion.
[24] *Equites,* vs. 1085, *Vespae,* vs. 380, and *Aves,* vs. 988.
[25] Plutarch, *Agesilaus,* 3.

by the seer Diopeithes. According to the biographer Satyros, Anaxagoras was accused by Thucydides, the son of Melesias, the chief political adversary of Pericles; but according to Plutarch, Diopeithes was the accuser.[26] Probably the two worked together. Diopeithes carried a law in the popular assembly authorizing trials of persons who did not believe in the divine and who disseminated teachings about the celestial phenomena. Here we find the kernel of the matter, the clash between the old religion and the new philosophy. The heavenly bodies were mythological gods who had hardly any cult. The contention that the sun was a glowing lump and the moon another inhabited world could hardly be counted as atheism. On the other hand such celestial phenomena as eclipses had a very important place as omens in the art of the seers. The seers became aware of the danger to their art, which some people had already begun to doubt, of the physical explanation of such phenomena.

Another story about the seer Lampon which is told by Plutarch is very illuminating in regard to the situation.[27] A ram with one horn only was brought to Pericles. According to the notions of the ancients this was an ominous portent. Lampon interpreted it to mean that of the two rivals in Athenian politics, Pericles and Thucydides, the one to whom this ram had been brought should carry the day. But Anaxagoras had the skull of the ram cut open and showed that the brain had the form of an egg with its small end turned toward the root of the single horn. He gave a physical explanation of the portent. Plutarch adds that the people admired the sagacity of Anaxagoras much but shortly afterward, when Thucydides had been ostracized, that of Lampon much more.

The moderns generally think that the clash took place be-

---

[26] Diogenes Laertius, II, 12 ff.; Plutarch, *Pericles,* 32.
[27] *Pericles,* 6.

tween the old religion and the criticism advanced by the Sophists. This view is at best one-sided. A very severe criticism of the gods and of their cult had been made by Xenophanes and Heraclitus without doing much harm. The Sophists, in fact, were not so aggressive as these philosophers, although their criticism without doubt undermined faith in the gods. Critias advanced the opinion that some wise man had invented the gods in order to deter men from doing wrong in secret.[28] Prodicus took up the metonymical use of the names of the gods which was already common in Homer and concluded that man considered as a god everything that was useful to him and that hence wine was called Dionysus, fire Hephaistos, bread Demeter, and so forth.[29] Protagoras was cautious, stating that he was not able to say of the gods whether they existed or not, nor what shape they had; he said that much prevents knowing this—the obscurity of the matter and the brevity of human life.[30] This is philosophy and must be passed over in an exposition of popular religion. The discussions of the Sophists were beyond the horizon of the common people, who listened to them partly in amusement and partly in irritation. It is characteristic that Euripides, the spokesman of the new wisdom on the stage, won few victories, while many fell to Sophocles. Sophocles won the favor of the people because he was a good Athenian citizen who believed in the gods. But his religion was conventional, if this word is not taken in a bad sense. It is very characteristic that the only part of religion for which he shows genuine zeal is the belief in oracles.

The intellectual arguments of the Sophists were above the understanding of the common people. The arguments of natural philosophy, at least to a certain degree, were not. Aris-

[28] *Sisyphus,* in Nauck, *Tragicorum Graecorum fragmenta,* pp. 771 ff.
[29] Frag. 5, in Diels, *Fragmente der Vorsokratiker,* II, 316.
[30] Frag. 4, in Diels, *Fragmente der Vorsokratiker,* II, 265.

tophanes popularized them. In *The Clouds* he makes Socrates prove that Zeus does not exist by the fact that the thunderbolt hits not the wrongdoers but temples, mountaintops, and tall oaks. This the people understood. In another passage he gives a grotesque explanation of the rain which Zeus pours down.[31]

Moderns are astonished that natural philosophy and sophistic are confused, that Aristophanes makes Socrates represent them both. From the point of view of the good Athenian citizen it is not astonishing at all. They were not so educated or lettered as to be able to distinguish between the hairsplitting of the Sophists and the hypotheses of the natural philosophers, of whose doctrines the Sophists were not ignorant. The people confused them, and Aristophanes reflects popular opinion by doing the same, although his exposition of their doctrines in *The Clouds* was a little too much for the audience. This comedy was not a success.

The real clash took place between that part of religion which interfered most in practical life and with which everyone came in contact every day, namely, the art of foretelling the future, and the attempts of natural philosophy to give physical explanations of celestial and atmospheric phenomena, of portents, and of other events. Such explanations undermined the belief in the art of the seers and made it superfluous. For if these phenomena were to be explained in a natural way, the art of the seers came to naught. Belief in the oracles also was weakened. The prejudices shown by the oracles, as in the case of the favor shown by the Delphic oracle for the Spartans, contributed to the disbelief. The belief in the oracles was the business not only of the priests and seers but also of the politicians. Only one method of foretelling the future—dreams —was not attacked. Everyone believed in dreams, and even

---

[31] *Nubes,* vss. 399 ff.

Aristotle treated of the divine nature of dreams.[32] Everyone
wanted to look into the future, as people still do. The defense
of the oracles and of the art of the seers was a very important
matter.

Naturally the seers and interpreters of oracles and omens
defended their art, and since their art was implied in the old
religion, the defense of the old religion also fell to their lot.
For the real point where belief and disbelief clashed was the
opposition between the art of foretelling the future and the
physical explanations of natural philosophy. The clash occurred not in intellectual discussion but in practical life, and
consequently it became the business of the whole people. That
it was so is proved by the fact that the seers rose up to defend
the old religion when they became aware of the danger.
Diopeithes introduced the trials for atheism, and the first
man to be accused was Anaxagoras, the Ionian natural philosopher who lived at Athens. The denunciation of Socrates
contained the same accusation, that he searched for things
beneath the earth and above the sky. But in his case a reference to sophistic was added, for he was also accused of making
the weaker case appear the stronger.

The trials for atheism were useless. They were not able
to check the increasing disbelief, and they ceased in the course
of time. They are no honor to Athens, but we should try to
understand the situation from which they arose. This situation
was created by the interference of religion in practical life
and politics, and it explains why men who were at the same
time politicians and seers thought it possible to dispel the
danger by means of laws and courts. They were supported by
the Athenian people, for the people disliked the attacks on
the gods who had given glory and power to their city and in
emergencies they feared the wrath of these gods. Disbelief in

[32] *On Dreams* and *On Prophecy in Sleep.*

the gods was manifest in the physical explanations of the phenomena of nature, which the seers interpreted as signs of the wrath of the gods. The people understood this, and the trials for atheism were the consequence. The fate of the old religion was sealed, but the belief in the art of foretelling the future did not cease. In late antiquity it was stronger than ever. It was a part of popular religion, and I have wished to put its importance in the right light.

I have tried to expound the popular religion of the ancient Greeks. To many popular religion is religion in folklore, and I have dwelt at length on this part of the religion. The great gods also have their roots in popular religion, although they come to us magnified by art and literature. Certain moral and social ideas formed a part of the life of the people, and these also found religious expression and were placed under the protection of the gods. They are an important part of popular religion.

Religion is dependent on the conditions of life. When these change new needs arise and old forms wane, and popular religion undergoes corresponding changes. Such changes were effected when people crowded into the towns and began to earn their livelihood not by agriculture and stockbreeding but by industry and commerce. Changes in political life and the rise of democracy also caused certain changes in religion. We should bear in mind that in the democratic states the people formed the popular assembly to which all decisions pertained, even in religious matters. The result was that religion was secularized to a certain degree. But it was not dead. Religion tried to find new forms corresponding to the new needs and the new ideas of the people. This movement was only beginning in the fifth and fourth centuries B.C. The real turning point is the age of the Sophists. It came to an issue in late antiquity.

I take the liberty to conclude with a simile. Religion is like a grove with tall and stately trees, which reach the sky and strike the eye from afar, and with an undergrowth of brushwood and grass. It is easy to fell the trees, and, like the pines in the proverb which King Croesus referred to when he threatened to eradicate the Milesians like a pine, they do not put forth new shoots, although new trees can be planted instead of the old ones. But the undergrowth persists. The brushwood and the grass may be cut down or even burned off; it springs up again. Every year the undergrowth brings forth the same simple leaves and blossoms. It changes only if the mother soil is changed. This took place in ancient Greece, as it does today, through the rise of new conditions of life, industry, commerce, democracy, and intercourse between peoples and classes. Popular religion changed accordingly. In backward parts of the country, however, the old mode of life and the old popular religion persisted and have continued to persist down to our own day, but they are giving way again because conditions of life are once more being profoundly changed.

ILLUSTRATIONS

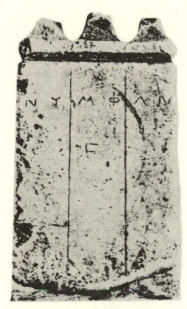

2. ARCADIAN HERM   3. HERMES PSYCHOPOMPOS

4. HERM OFFERING

5. GOAT DAEMONS

6. RIVER GOD

7. VOTIVE MASKS

8. PAN AND NYMPHS

9. LANDSCAPE WITH SHRINES

10. HERO IN A SHRINE

11. KERNOS

12. SWINGING FESTIVAL

13. DIONYSUS IN A SHIP

14. WINE OFFERING TO DIONYSUS

15. INITIATION RITES

16. GODS OF ELEUSIS

17. ANODOS OF PHEREPHATTA

18. ANODOS OF KORE

19. BEARDED TRIPTOLEMOS

20. CORN IN A SHRINE

21. REUNION OF DEMETER AND KORE

22. DEPARTURE OF TRIPTOLEMOS

23. TRIPTOLEMOS WITH A PLOW

24. THE CHILD PLOUTON

25. PLOUTON AND PERSEPHONE (PHEREPHATTA)

26. ZEUS KTESIOS

27. ZEUS MEILICHIOS

28. ZEUS MEILICHIOS

29. DIOSCURI

30. **APOLLO**
AGYIEUS

31. DIOSCURI

32. DIOSCURI COMING TO A MEAL

33. TRIPLE HECATE

[154]

34. ATHENA ERGANE

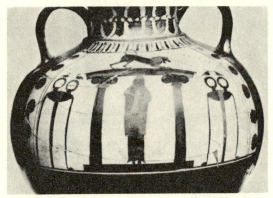

Courtesy of the British Museum

35. CYBELE, THE GREAT MOTHER

Courtesy of the British Museum

36. BENDIS

37. OFFERING TO ASCLEPIUS

38. ASCLEPIUS OF MELOS 39. GARDENS OF ADONIS

INDEX

INDEX

Acheloos, 11

Acquirer, the, epithet of Zeus, 67, 70

Actaeon, 113

Acts, ancient Greek piety expressed in, 73, 76

Adam, James, 3

Adonis, 96 f., 131

Aeschines, 93, 97*n*; quoted, 74

Aeschylus, 68, 70, 108; *Agamemnon,* 109

Agathos Daimon, 33, 70, 73

Agriculture, pastoral life, 5 ff.; understanding of Greek popular religion must start from, 5; climatic conditions and crops, 6, 51; customs and festivals, 22-41; importance of, 22, 57; basis of Eleusinian Mysteries an agrarian cult, 42, 45, 49, 54, 57 ff.; idea that civilized and peaceful life is created by, 57 ff.

Agyieus, *see* Apollo Agyieus

Aiora, festival, 33

Alcibaides, 122, 131, 133

All Souls' Day, 31, 34

Alms, customs of asking for, 37, 38

Ammon, 92, 124, 131

Amphictyonies, 98

Anaktes (the Dioscuri), 69

Anaxagoras, 122, 134, 137

Animal sacrifice, 87; meaning and origin, 74 f.

Animal-shaped daemons, 10-13

Anthesteria, festival, 31, 33 f., 35

Anthropology and study of religion, 3

Apocalypse of St. Peter, 119

Apollo, 9, 10, 15, 23, 39, 47, 98, 103, 108, 112; Thargelia dedicated to, 27; as averter of evil, 79 f.; god of healing, 93; ritualism which he promoted

concerned only with cult, 106, 107; *see also* Delphic oracle

Apollo Agyieus, 80, 82

Apollo Patroos, 67, 82, 83

Apulian tomb vases, 55, 119

Apulunas, 79

Arcadian deities, 9, 10

Archedemos, 14, 16

Archilochus, quoted, 74

Archons, newly elected, 66-67, 82

Ares, 112

Aristophanes, 36, 66, 80, 87, 91, 93, 94, 96, 97, 100, 111, 122; references to Eleusinian Mysteries, 58, 59; attitude toward seers and oracles, 132, 133; exposition of natural philosophy, 136; *The Birds,* 132; *The Clouds,* 136; *The Frogs,* 118; *The Knights,* 132; *The Peace,* 92

Aristotle, 4*n*, 23, 86, 122, 137

Armistice during festivals, 99

Artemis, 15 ff., 18, 21, 30, 39, 65; foremost of the nymphs, 16, 17; epithets, 16

Artisans and their deities, 87-90

Asclepius, 20, 95, 121; cults and sanctuary, 93 f.

Astrology, 106

Atheism, trials for, 94, 133, 137

Athena, 32, 35, 47, 60, 61, 81, 132; holy snake of, 72; epithet Phratria, 83; temple, 86; protectress of artisans, 88 f.

Athens, praised as cradle of civilization, 56; leadership in commerce and culture, 86; patriotism and piety, 86 f.

Autumn festivals, 24-26, 42, 46, 49; *see also* Thesmophoria

Bacchos, 47, 62, 96; *see also* Dionysus
Bacchylides, 69
Bacis, oracles of, 127, 129
Baptism in cult of Kotyto, 93
Bendis, 92
Birds, The, 132
Birth of child, representations of, 61
Brotherhood of humanity, 58, 63
Bucoliasts, 30, 37
Bucolic poetry, 30, 36, 37

Cabiri, the, 92, 121
Calendars, 23, 106
Campbell, Lewis, 3
Carnea, festival, 35; armistice during, 99
Celestial phenomena, physical explanation of, 134 ff.
Centaurs, 12, 13
Chalkeia, festival, 89
Charon, 116
Child, birth of, in art, 61
Choes, festival, 33-34
Chresmologoi, the, 127
Christianity, swept away the great gods, 16; Greek religion and, 20, 31, 73, 75, 76, 100
Christmas, resemblance to Anthesteria, 34
Chytroi, festival, 31, 34
Circle, magic, 28
Cities, so-called, often villages, 5, 22; religion of, 84-101; life and conditions in, 84 ff.; country population crowded into, unemployment, 84; lead in culture, 84, 85; home of the great gods, 85 ff.; great temples, 86; artisans, 87-89; foreign gods brought in, 90 ff.; skepticism and emotionalism, 94-97; panegyreis, 97-101
Citizenship, proof of, 67, 82
Cleisthenes, 82
Clement of Alexandria, 43, 50; quoted, 45
Climatic conditions, and crops, 6, 51
Clouds, The, 136
Comedy, origin of, 36
Coppersmiths, 88, 89
Corn, as wealth, 51; in Eleusinian rites, 55
Corn deities, 24, 51, 52; *see also* Demeter; Kore

Cornucopia, 47, 61, 69
Crafts and their deities, 87-90
Critias, 135
Crops, relation to climate, 51; *see also* Agriculture
Cult places, *see* Sanctuaries
Cults, care of, 80-83
Cumont, F., 119
Curses on leaden tablets, 114

Daemons, nature, 10 ff.
Danaids, the, 116
Days, The, 105 f.
De-, significance of, 24, 51
Dead, the, beliefs about, 8; offerings to, 8, 30, 34; abode of, 9, 59, 64, 115-20; souls represented by snake, 71; cult of, 115 ff.; *see also* Ghosts; Heroes
Death, ideas evoked by Eleusinian Mysteries, 59, 63
Deisidaimonia, 110
Delphi, 86, 93, 98, 116, 117
Delphic oracle, 20, 23, 57, 123, 128, 130, 133, 136; attitude toward legalism and mysticism, 106-8; popularity based on ability to foretell future, 124
Demeter, 23, 27, 32, 92, 98, 104, 135; goddess of cereals, 24, 50, 52n; rites and festivals, 24 ff., 33, 36; Mysteries of, 32, 45; a goddess of the religion of Eleusis, 46 ff.; myth of the rape of daughter of, 48 ff.; Ploutos born of Iasion and, 51, 62; reunion with Kore, 54-55
Democritus, quoted, 118
Demosthenes, 93, 97n, 114
Descent of Kore, festival, 52; *see also* Kore
Diagoras, 122
Diet, staple, 22, 32
Dieterich, A., 119
Dionysiac orgies, 95, 103
Dionysus, 13, 32, 35, 39, 60, 93, 135; festivals, 23, 33, 34, 35 ff., 47, 86; Mysteries of, 31, 32, 50; date, functions, 35; costume, 47; mixing up of cult of, with Mysteries of Eleusis, 48, 62; popularity as herald of mystic and ecstatic religion, 103

Diopeithes, 133; trials initiated by, 134, 137

Dioscuri, the, 60, 68 f., 72

Disease, healers of, 20, 93 f., 95; superstitions relating to, 111 ff.

Dörpfeld, W., 79

Drama, origin in rural customs, 36

Dreams, belief in, 124, 125, 136

Earthquakes, 11

Eiresione, 29, 36, 39; see also May bough

Eleusinian Mysteries, 7, 25, 31, 39, 42-64, 95, 99, 116; basis of, an agrarian cult, 42, 45, 49, 54; secret rites, 42 ff.; akin to the Thesmophoria, 42, 44, 46, 49; treatment by Christian authors, 43; belonged to Eumolpidae, 43, 46, 81; modern attempts to find out kernel of, 44; antiquity and persistence of, 46, 63; mixed with cult of Dionysus, 48, 62; kernel of, the ascent of Corn Maiden, 54; deeper ideas of life and death evoked by, 59, 63; trials for profanation of, 94, 122

Eleusis, religion of, 42-64; antiquity of cult, 46, 63; deities, 46 ff., 60; founded upon idea of agriculture as creating civilized and peaceful life, 57

Emotional religion, 95-97

Empedocles, 99

Encirclement, magical rite, 28

Enodia, name for Hecate, 91

Epidaurus, sanctuary at, 86, 93, 94, 113

Epilepsy, 111 f.

Ergane, 89; see also Athena

Erichthonios, 61

Eternity of life, 60, 63, 64

Eubouleus, 47, 48, 49

Eumolpidae, family of the, 43, 46, 81

Euripides, 59, 135

Europe, northern: similarities between beliefs and customs of Greece and, 12, 13, 26, 29, 37, 41, 71

Euthymus, 18

Evans, Sir Arthur, 71

Evil, averters of, 78 ff.

Exegetes, the, 111, 133

Fairs at panegyreis, 100

Families, cults under care of, 46, 81

Family and house cults, 65-83

Family, the model and basis of state organization, 75

Farnell, L. R., 20

Father, epithet of Zeus, 70, 77

Female, see Women

Fence, house, 65, 66

Fertility, festivals and magic, 25, 26, 27, 29, 33, 34, 36, 49

Festivals, rural, 22-41; Eleusinian Mysteries originally an autumn festival, 42, 49; of cities, 87, 89, 92, 97 ff.; women's part in, 96; the panegyreis, 97-101

First fruits, offering of, 27 ff.

Fleece, 7

Flowers, festival of, 33 f., 35; crown of, 40

Folklore, connection with religion, 40, 72, 110

Food of Greeks, 22, 32

Foreigners and strangers, 58, 73, 77

Foreign gods brought into Greece, 90, 91 ff.

Foretelling of the future, 123 ff.; see also Oracles and Seers

Frazer, Sir James, 3

Frogs, The, 118; quoted, 58

Fruits, as food, 22, 32; festivals and offerings, 27 ff., 30, 36

Furtwängler, A., 62

Future, foretelling of the, 123 ff.; see also Oracles and Seers

Games, the great, 97-101

Ge, 62

Generations, eternity of life through, 60, 63

Genetyllis, 96

Ghosts, heroes as, 18, 112; lamia and other specters, 91; goddess of, 111; see also Heroes

Goatlike daemons, 10, 12, 13

"God, the," 46, 47, 48

"Goddess, the," 46, 47, 48

Gods, see Great gods; also under name, e.g., Apollo; Demeter

Golden Fleece, 7

Goldsmiths, 88, 89

Good Daemon, 70, 73

Gorgias, 99
Gospel of St. John, excerpt, 59
Great Dionysia, 36, 86
Great gods, outlived by minor deities, 16, 18, 21, 41; religion in cities, 85 ff.; as state gods became remote from men, 87, 121
Great Mother, 91, 92, 112

Hades, 9, 59, 115, 116, 119
Haloa, festival, 32-33
Harrison, Jane, 3, 74
Harvest festivals, 26 ff.
Healers of disease, 20, 93 f., 95, 112, 113
Hearth, sanctity of, 72 f., 75 ff.; role in public cult, 75
Hecate, 80, 111, 112, 115; origin, cult, 90 f.; devotion of women to, 97
Hell, beliefs concerning, 118-20
Hephaistos, 89, 135
Heracles, 60, 78; difference between Theseus and, 57
Heraclitus, 135
Herkeios, epithet of Zeus, 66-67, 78, 82, 83
Hermes, 8, 9, 10, 21, 53, 61, 62, 115
Herms, 8, 9, 18; trials for smashing of, 94, 122
Herodotus 72, 73, 81, 85, 109; biography of Homer attributed to, 37, 88; oracles and presages related by, 124, 128, 129
Heroes, nature of, functions, 18 ff., 21; ghost stories about, 18, 112; tombs and sanctuaries, 19; similarity to saints, 20; in Eleusinian religion, 47, 60; as gods of healing, 93
Hesiod, cited, 10, 35, 51, 65, 74, 85, 108, 110; references to Demeter, 24; ideal of peace and justice, 57; rules for religious life and conduct of man, 104 ff.; origin, 104; *Theogony,* 90; *Works and Days,* 104 ff.
Hestia, 72, 73, 76; position and importance of, 75
Hierocles, 133
Hieron, skyphos by, 56*n*
Hippocrates, *De morbo sacro,* 111 f., 113
Holy disease, 111 f.

Homer, cited, 12, 15, 19, 21, 24, 26, 35, 51, 59, 65, 66, 78, 88, 89, 93, 110, 116, 117, 135; biography of, attributed to Herodotus, 37, 88; sanctuaries described by, 81, 86; called creator of the gods, 85
Homeric Hymn to Demeter, 51, 56, 90; references to the Eleusinian cult, 43, 45, 58; myth of the rape of Demeter's daughter, 48, 49
Homeric Hymn to Hermes, 9, 10, 65
Horse-shaped daemons, 11-13
House and family cults, 65-83
Houses, described, 65 f.; hearth, 72
Hrozný, B., 79
Human sacrifice, 6, 18, 113
Hunting, goddess of, 15
Hybris, conception of, 108 f.
Hyperborean virgins, 38
Hysteria, religious, 94, 122

Iacchos, 47, 54, 62
Iasion, 51, 62
Icarius, 33
Immortality, beliefs concerning, 60, 63, 64, 116
Impiety, trials for, 94, 122, 133, 137
Imprecations on leaden tablets, 114 f.
Initiation rites, Eleusinian, 45, 49
Isocrates, 56
Isthmia, games, 98

Jugs, Festival of the, 33-34
Jupiter, 70; *see also* Zeus
Justice, problem of, 77, 108 f.; retributive, 117

Kalamaia, festival, 26
Kallias, cited, 56
Karneia festival, 35; armistice during, 99
Kataibates, epithet of Zeus, 67
Katharmoi, 99
Kephisodotos, statue of "Peace" by, 61, 62
Kernos, 31
Kipling, Rudyard, quoted, 71
Knights, The, 132
Kolias, 96
Kollyba, 31

Kore, Corn Maiden, 24, 32; as Eleusinian goddess, 46 ff.; myth of rape by Plouton, 48 ff.; aspects referring to life and to death, 53; reunion with Corn Mother, 54; *see also* Persephone
Kotyto, 93
Ktesios, epithet of Zeus, 67-69, 78
Kykeon, 45, 49, 50

Lakrateides, 48
Lamia, 91
Lampon, 133, 134
Lang, Andrew, 3
Laurel branch, 39
Leagues for protection of sanctuaries, 98
Legalism, 103 ff.
Life, ideas of, evoked by Eleusinian Mysteries, 59, 63
Lightning, god of, 67
Loaf offered as first fruit, 27, 28
Lovatelli, Countess, 49
Lunar month, 106
Lying in the mud, 116, 118, 120
Lysimachides, relief by, 46

Magic, weather, 6, 7; fertility, 25, 27, 29, 33, 34, 49; purificatory, 27-28; as cure for diseases, 112; Plato's attitude toward, 113; widespread belief in, 115; *see also* Witchcraft and sorcery
Magna Mater, *see* Great Mother
Marathonian tetrapolis, calendar, 19
Masks, votive, 16
Masses, fate of religion determined by, 4
Mater dolorosa, Greek (Demeter), 54
Maximus of Tyre, 23
May bough, 29, 36; customs, 37, 39 f.; symbolism, 38
Meals, sanctity of, 73 f.
Meat, 22
Megaron, described, 66; hearth, 72
Meilichios, epithet of Zeus, 69-70
Melanaigis, epithet of Dionysus, 36
Menander, 68
Miraculous healings, 95
Modern and ancient customs, 23, 26, 37, 38, 41, 71, 72, 100, 110
Modern research, 3 ff.

Moirai, the, 14
Monsters, 91
Morality associated with agriculture, 58, 63
Mostellaria, 113
Mountains, 6, 7, 8, 17
Mud, lying in the, 116, 118, 120
Mystic and ecstatic cults, 63, 95, 97, 103, 108; *see also* Eleusinian Mysteries

Natural philosophy, clash with religion, 134-38
Nature spirits or gods, 5-21
Nemea, games, 98
Nemesis, conception of, 108 f.
Nicias, 126, 132
Ninnion, tablet of, 54, 60
Nobility, the, 82, 84
Nymphs, 11, 13-17, 18

Odyssey, 59, 117
Olives, 32
Olympia, sanctuary at, 86, 98, 99
Olympic games, 98, 99
Omens, belief in, 123 ff.; *see also* Oracles
Onomacritus, 128
Oracles and seers, 123-38; military dependence upon, 125, 130; questions to, 125; political role, 127, 130; collections of oracles, 129; critics of, 129, 130; causes that undermined belief in, 136 f.
Orestes, 18, 19, 113
Orgeones, 82
Orgiastic cults, 93, 95, 97
Orphism, 103, 116, 117, 119, 128
Oschophoria, festival, 25, 34, 35
Otto, W. F., 4

Pan, 10, 13, 14, 17, 96
Panagia Euangelistria, 95
Panegyreis, 97-101; religious significance, 97, 100; sanctuaries, 98; importance, national and cultural, 99
Panegyricus, 56
Pankarpia, 30, 68
Panspermia, 30 f., 68
Pasios, epithet of Zeus, 67
Pastoral life and religion, 5-21, 22-41
Pausanias, cited, 56, 99

Peace, The, 92

Peasants, customs and religion, 5 ff., 22 ff.

Persephone, 47, 48, 53, 61; varying forms of name, 53; two aspects referring to life and to death, 53; *see also* Kore

Peterich, E., 4

Phallus, 36

Pharmakos, 27, 28

Pherephatta, 53

Philologists, research by, 3

Philosophy, natural, 134-38

Phoenix of Colophon, 38

Phratries, 82

Piety, expression of, by Greeks and moderns, 73, 76

Pindar, cited, 59, 92

Pisistratus, 36, 86, 128

Pitza, cave at, 14

Plato, religious importance, 4; attitude toward magic and magicians, 113 f.; influence of accounts of the other world, 119; *Republic,* 118

Plautus, *Mostellaria,* 113

Plouton, 47, 48, 51, 52, 61, 62; myth of the rape of Demeter's daughter by, 48 ff.

Ploutos, 51, 61, 62

Plutarch, 36, 42, 97, 126, 131, 134

Politics, *see* State

Polycrates, 109

Polygnotus, picture at Delphi, by, 116, 117

Pompeian frescoes, 17

Poseidon, 11, 18, 21, 81, 88, 112

Potters and their deities, 87-90

Poverty and social distress, age of, 84, 102

Prayer, in words and in acts, 73

Presages, belief in, 123 ff.; *see also* Oracles and Seers

Priestesses, 96, 97n

Priesthood, 46, 80 f.

Primitive religion, 3, 5

Prodicus, 135

Profane and sacred intermingled, 40, 76, 100

Protagoras, 122, 135

Prudentius, 60

Psychosabbaton, the, 31

Punishment in the other world, 114-20

Purification a complement of legalism, 104

Purificatory rites, 27 f.

Pyanopsia, festival, 29, 36

Pythia, games, 98

Rain, prayer for, 6, 7

Relics, of saints and heroes, 20

Religion, modern investigations, 3 ff.; primitive elements, 3, 5; systematization, 4; popular, the most long-lived, 16, 18, 21, 32, 41, 139; Christian and Greek forms, 20, 31, 73, 75, 76, 100; connection with folklore, 40, 72, 110; sacred and secular intermingled, 40, 76, 100; Eleusinian Mysteries the finest bloom of Greek popular, 42; power and persistence of the most venerable, 63; ancient and modern expressions of piety compared, 73, 76; social aspect, 80 ff., 101; unity of state and, 80, 86, 123, 137; criticism by Sophists and others, 94, 122, 133, 135 f.; trials for impiety, 94, 122, 133, 137; emotional, of women, 95-97; age in which new movements originated, 102; two main streams of contrasting ideas, 103; encounters political life and the new enlightenment, 121 ff.; clash with natural philosophy, 134-38; dependence on, and change with, conditions of life, 138

Republic, 118

Retributive justice, 117

Ritualism, 105, 107; *see also* Legalism

Rivers, gods and spirits, 10 f.

Rohde, Erwin, 103

Rural, life and religion, 5-21; sanctuaries, 14, 18, 81, 86; customs and festivals, 22-41

Rustic Dionysia, 36

Sabazios, a form of Dionysus, 93, 96, 110, 121

Sacred and profane intermingled, 40, 76, 100

Sacrifice, animal, 87; meaning and origin, 74 f.

Sacrifice, human, 6, 18, 113

Saints, similarity of heroes to, 20

Salaminioi, inscription of, 19

Sanctity, inherent in the place, 76
Sanctuaries, rustic, 14, 18, 81, 86; the temples, 46, 80, 81, 85 f., 87; of panegyreis, 98
Satyrs, 12, 13
Sea, deities, 11, 14, 92
Secular and sacred intermingled, 40, 76, 100
Seers and oracles, 123-38; see also Oracles and Seers
Seilenoi, 12-13
Seven Sages, 108
Sexual symbols in Eleusinian Mysteries, 44
Shrines, see Sanctuaries
Sibylline Books, 129
Sickness, healers of, 20, 93 f., 95; superstitions relating to, 111 ff.
Skirophoria, festival, 25
Slaves admitted to Eleusinian Mysteries, 58
Smith, W. Robertson, 74
Snake, in house cult, 67-72; gods in guise of or represented by, 67-72; souls of dead represented by, 71; Minoan snake-goddess, 71; in cult of Athena, 72
Social aspect of religion, 80 ff., 101
Social distress and poverty, 84, 102
Social justice, problem of, 77, 108 f.
Socrates, 136; so-called prison of, 14; trial, 122, 137
Solon, 82, 117
Sophists, 99; attacks against religion, 94, 122, 133, 135 f.; views of, confused with natural philosophy, 136
Sophocles, 58, 66, 88; made a hero under name of Dexion, 94; religious beliefs, 135
Sorcery, see Witchcraft and sorcery
Soter, epithet of Zeus, 70
Soul, the, 116
Specters, 91; see also Ghosts
State and religion, 80, 86, 123, 137; role of oracles, 127 ff.
Stone heaps, 8; see also Herms
Stones, cult of, 79 f.
Strabo, on ancient landscape, 17 f.
Strangers and foreigners, 58, 73, 77
Superstition, defined, 110; distinguished from religion, 110 f.; amount of, beliefs, 111 ff.

Suppliants, 77
Swine, 25, 49
Swinging festival, 33

Tabellae defixionis, 114 f.
Telemachos of Acharnae, 94
Temesa, hero of, 18, 113
Temples, 80, 81; rustic sanctuaries, 14, 18, 81, 86; Mycenaean mystery hall, 46; the great temples, 85 f., 87
Thallophoroi on Parthenon frieze, 40
Thalysia, festival, 24, 26 f., 29, 30
Thargelia, festival, 27 f., 29, 37
Theocritus, 26
Theogony, 90
Theology, 4
Theophrastus, 79, 110
Theseus, 19; functions of, 57
Thesmophoria, festival, 24-26, 32; links with Eleusinian Mysteries, 42, 44, 46, 49
Thetis, 14
Thucydides, 65; attitude toward oracles, 130, 131
Thucydides, statesman, 134
Thunder, 6, 67
Tisamenus, 127
Tomb cult, 115
Towns, see Cities
Tragedy, origin of, 36
Tree cult and nymphs, 14, 16
Trials for impiety, 94, 122, 133, 137
Triptolemos, 47, 55 f., 57, 60, 61
Truces during festivals, 99
Tyrants, rule of, 85, 86

Underworld, beliefs concerning, 9, 59, 64, 115-20

Valmin, M. N., 66n
Vari, cave at, 14, 16
Vegetation, deities, 35, 50; connection of Kore myth with, 50; cycle represented by Adonis, 96; see also Agriculture
Vesta, 72; see also Hestia
Villages, 5, 22
Virgins, 28, 38, 96
Viticulture, 32; festivals, 32 ff.
Votive masks, 16

War, heroes helpful in, 19; part played by oracles and seers, 125, 130

Water, deities, 10 f., 12, 14
Wayfarers, 8
Wealth, god of, 51, 61; corn as, 51
Weather god, 6-8
Weather magic, 6, 7
Wilamowitz-Moellendorff, U. von, 3
Wine, festivals, 32 ff.; god of, 35
Witchcraft and sorcery, 78, 80, 111, 114, 115; goddess of, 90, 91, 97, 111
Women, religion of, 14, 15, 95-97; festivals of Demeter celebrated by, 25; subordinate position of, 96
Works and Days, 104
Writers, expression of religious thought, 3 f.

Xenophanes, 135
Xenophon, 79, 110; belief in oracles and presages, 123 f., 126, 127

Zeus, 24, 32, 50, 57, 82, 86, 89, 104, 105, 107; as weather god, 6-8, 21, 67, 136; as god of house and family, 66 ff.; epithets of, 66 ff., 83; in guise of snake, 67, 68, 69, 71 f.; the Dioscuri sons of, 68, 72; as father, 70, 77; as protector, 77 f., 108; change in status of, 78
Zeus Akraios, 7
Zeus Herkeios, 66-67, 78, 82, 83
Zeus Kataibates, 67
Zeus Ktesios, 67-69, 78
Zeus Laphystios, 6, 7
Zeus Lykaios, 6
Zeus Maimaktes, 7
Zeus Meilichios, 69-70
Zeus Melosios, 7
Zeus Panhellenios, 7
Zeus Soter, 70

Pennsylvania Paperbacks

PP01 Fauset, Arthur H. BLACK GODS OF THE METROPOLIS *Negro Religious Cults of the Urban North* With a New Introduction by John Szwed

PP02 Bohm, David CAUSALITY AND CHANCE IN MODERN PHYSICS

PP03 Warner, Sam Bass THE PRIVATE CITY *Philadelphia in Three Periods of Its Growth*

PP04 Bestor, Arthur BACKWOODS UTOPIAS *The Sectarian and the Owenite Phase of Communitarian Socialism in America, 1663–1829*

PP05 Cochran, Thomas C., and Ruben E. Reina CAPITALISM IN ARGENTINE CULTURE *A Study of Torcuato Di Tella and S. I. A. M.*

PP06 Saunders, E. Dale BUDDHISM IN JAPAN *With an Outline of Its Origins in India*

PP07 Lumiansky, Robert M., and Herschel Baker, Editors CRITICAL APPROACHES TO SIX MAJOR ENGLISH WORKS *Beowulf through Paradise Lost*

PP08 Morris, Clarence, Editor THE GREAT LEGAL PHILOSOPHERS *Selected Readings in Jurisprudence*

PP09 Patai, Raphael SOCIETY, CULTURE AND CHANGE IN THE MIDDLE EAST

PP10 Jaspers, Karl PHILOSOPHY OF EXISTENCE, Tr. and with an Introduction by Richard F. Grabau

PP11 Goffman, Erving STRATEGIC INTERACTION

PP12 Birdwhistell, Ray L. KINESICS AND CONTEXT *Essays on Body Motion Communication*

PP13 Glassie, Henry PATTERN IN THE MATERIAL FOLK CULTURE OF THE EASTERN UNITED STATES

PP14 Hodgen, Margaret T. EARLY ANTHROPOLOGY IN THE SIXTEENTH AND SEVENTEENTH CENTURIES

PP15 Webber, Melvin, et al. EXPLORATIONS INTO URBAN STRUCTURE

PP16 Bernstein, Richard J. PRAXIS AND ACTION *Contemporary Philosophies of Human Activity*

PP17 Peters, Edward, Editor THE FIRST CRUSADE *The Chronicle of Fulcher of Chartres and Other Source Materials*

PP18 Lewin, Julius STUDIES IN AFRICAN LAW

PP19 Anscombe, G. E. M. AN INTRODUCTION TO WITTGENSTEIN'S *TRACTATUS*

PP20 Boisen, Anton T. THE EXPLORATION OF THE INNER WORLD *A Study of Mental Disorder and Religious Experience*

PP21 Cornford, Francis M. THUCYDIDES MYTHISTORICUS

PP22 Hegel, G. W. F. EARLY THEOLOGICAL WRITINGS, Tr. by T. M. Knox and Richard Kroner, Introduction by Richard Kroner

PP23 Paton, H. J. THE CATEGORICAL IMPERATIVE *A Study in Kant's Moral Philosophy*

PP24 Peters, Edward, Editor CHRISTIAN SOCIETY AND THE CRUSADES 1198–1229 *Sources in Translation, including the Capture of Damietta by Oliver of Paderborn*

PP25 Kant, Immanuel THE DOCTRINE OF VIRTUE, Tr. by Mary Gregor, Introduction by H. J. Paton

PP26 Wishy, Bernard THE CHILD AND THE REPUBLIC *The Dawn of Modern American Child Nurture*

PP27 Moore, John C. LOVE IN TWELFTH-CENTURY FRANCE

PP28 Humboldt, Wilhelm v. LINGUISTIC VARIABILITY AND INTELLECTUAL DEVELOPMENT

PP29 Harbage, Alfred AS THEY LIKED IT *A Study of Shakespeare's Moral Artistry*

PP30 Morris, Clarence THE JUSTIFICATION OF THE LAW

PP31 Ossowska, Maria SOCIAL DETERMINANTS OF MORAL IDEAS

Pennsylvania Paperbacks continued

PP32 Beck, Aaron T. DEPRESSION *Causes and Treatment*
PP33 Nilsson, Martin P. HOMER AND MYCENAE
PP34 Nilsson, Martin P. GREEK FOLK RELIGION
PP35 Drew, Katherine Fischer THE BURGUNDIAN CODE *Book of Constitutions or Law of Gundobad/Additional Enactments*
PP36 Cassirer THE INDIVIDUAL AND THE COSMOS IN RENAISSANCE PHIL-OSOPHY
PP37 Guicciardini, Francesco MAXIMS AND REFLECTIONS
PP38 Frothingham, Octavius Brooks TRANSCENDENTALISM IN NEW ENGLAND *A History*